SERVICE IS FRONT STAGE

SERVICE IS FRONT STAGE

Positioning services for value advantage

James Teboul

INSEAD
Business Press

palgrave
macmillan

First published 2006 by
PALGRAVE MACMILLAN
Houndmills, Basingstoke, Hampshire RG21 6XS and
175 Fifth Avenue, New York, N.Y. 10010
Companies and representatives throughout the world

PALGRAVE MACMILLAN is the global academic imprint of the Palgrave Macmillan division of St. Martin's Press, LLC and of Palgrave Macmillan Ltd. Macmillan® is a registered trademark in the United States, United Kingdom and other countries. Palgrave is a registered trademark in the European Union and other countries.

ISBN-13: 978– 0–230–00660–7
ISBN-10: 0–230–00660–4

This book is printed on paper suitable for recycling and made from fully managed and sustained forest sources.

A catalogue record for this book is available from the British Library.

A catalog record for this book is available from the Library of Congress.

10   9   8   7   6   5   4   3   2   1
15 14 13 12 11 10 09 08 07 06

Printed and bound in Great Britain by
Creative Print & Design (Wales), Ebbw Vale

To Jean-Claude, Patrick and François

CONTENTS

List of Figures and Tables   **ix**

Introduction   **1**

1 Toward a new definition of services   **4**
The classic three-sector classification   4
A more detailed classification   7
Limits of these classifications   11
"Pure" services   12
We are all in services now, more or less   14
We shall be more and more in services in the future   16
Conclusion   17

2 Services: the front-stage experience   **19**
Identifying the service component   20
Front stage and back stage: two different worlds   23
Conclusion   29

3 The service triangle   **31**
From transaction to relationship   31
A dual-partnership culture   35
Turning the pyramid upside down   37
The service–profit chain   38
Power play on the service triangle   39
Conclusion   40

4 The service-intensity matrix   **41**
Product/outcome dimension   41
Intensity of interaction   42
The service-intensity matrix   43
The product/process matrix in the back stage   45
Positioning in the restaurant business   48
Positioning in e-business   50
Positioning in financial services   52
Positioning in book retailing   53
Positioning in consulting business   54
Conclusion   56

CONTENTS

5   **Finding and keeping the fit**   **57**
    Segmentation and focus   57
    Value to customer   58
    Value to employees   61
    Value to business   61
    The fit   62
    From service proposition to service delivery   63
    Commoditization and survival of the fittest   63
    The value creation cycle   64
    Creating elements of differentiation in the value creation cycle   67
    Conclusion   69

6   **Quality gaps**   **70**
    The design gap   70
    The delivery gap   71
    The perception gap   71
    The filters of perception   72
    Expectations   74
    The value gap   75
    Conclusion   76

7   **The three movements of quality**   **77**
    The first movement: everyone is responsible for doing the
      thing right   77
    The second movement: doing the right thing to satisfy the
      customer   85
    The third movement: the dynamics of process alignment   91
    Conclusion   98

8   **Balancing supply and demand**   **99**
    Managing demand   100
    Managing supply   103
    Yield or revenue management   106
    Managing waiting lines   108
    Conclusion   112

9   **From industrial to professional services**   **113**
    Industrial services   113
    Professional services   119

10 **Managing the change process**   **127**
    A simple analogy   129
    The four questions   129
    The three stages of implementation   134
    Conclusion   139

    Conclusion   **140**

Notes   143
Bibliography on services   146
Index   150

LIST OF FIGURES AND TABLES

Figures

1.1	Employment by sector in the United States	5
1.2	Service sector as a percentage of GDP (2003)	6
1.3	A more detailed classification of services	8
1.4	A black-box approach	12
1.5	Front stage	13
1.6	Back stage	14
1.7	From the industrial to the service sector	14
1.8	Three types of restaurant	15
1.9	Properties of information	16
1.10	Previous organizational structure	17
1.11	New organizational structure	17
2.1	The importance of the service component according to economic sector	20
2.2	Value creation cycle of a fish farmer	21
2.3	Performance leads, but service wins	22
2.4	The service triangle	28
2.5	Comparing products to services	29
3.1	The transactional approach	31
3.2	Marketing and selling a product	32
3.3	Marketing and selling a service	32
3.4	"Bow tie" relationship	33
3.5	Diamond relationship	33
3.6	Selling a simple product	34
3.7	Service transaction	34
3.8	Experience, transformation of client	35
3.9	Two partners on the same footing	36
3.10	Marketing and delivery symmetry	36
3.11	Extending the symmetry	37
3.12	Dual roles of managers	38
3.13	The service–profit chain	38
3.14	The service–profit triangle	39
3.15	Power play of the service triangle	40
4.1	The service-intensity matrix	41
4.2	Product dimension	42
4.3	Intensity of interaction	42
4.4	The service-intensity matrix	43

4.5	Accor hotels	44
4.6	Marriott hotels	44
4.7	Product/process matrix	45
4.8	Kitchen of a traditional restaurant	46
4.9	Fast-food production line	46
4.10	Flexibility in the back stage	47
4.11	Front-stage and back-stage matrices for the restaurant business	49
4.12	The service-intensity matrix for the restaurant business	50
4.13	Decreasing intensity of interaction	51
4.14	Trade-offs on the service-intensity matrix	52
4.15	Financial services on the service-intensity matrix	53
4.16	Book retailing on the service-intensity matrix	54
4.17	Consulting business on the service-intensity matrix	55
5.1	Value to the three stakeholders of the service triangle	58
5.2	Finding the fit for Benihana restaurants	60
5.3	Maximizing value to customers	60
5.4	Maximizing value to employees	61
5.5	Maximizing value to business	62
5.6	Value to the three stakeholders of the service triangle	63
5.7	Value creation cycle in the hotel business	65
5.8	Value creation cycle for budget hotels	65
5.9	Full-service hotel	66
5.10	Formule 1 hotels	67
5.11	Elements of differentiation for Virgin Atlantic	68
6.1	Design gap	70
6.2	Delivery gap	71
6.3	Perception gap	72
6.4	Filters of perception	74
6.5	Customer expectations	74
6.6	Value gap	75
6.7	The three quality gaps	76
7.1	Zero defects	77
7.2	Limits at 3σ	78
7.3	Limits at 6σ	79
7.4	Fishbone diagram for a back-stage process	80
7.5	Costs of nonconformance before and after investment in prevention	82
7.6	Fishbone diagram for a front-stage process	83
7.7	Process control at a call center	85
7.8	The proof of the pudding is in the eating	86
7.9	Squaring the circle	86
7.10	Maximizing value, influencing perception and expectations	86
7.11	Focusing on profitable customers	89
7.12	Value of a loyal customer	90
7.13	Customer and supply side of a business unit	92
7.14	Business process alignment	93
7.15	Processing of an insurance claim	94
7.16	Request for financing in IBM Credit Corporation	96
7.17	Process redesign for credit request processing	97
8.1	Demand versus supply	99
8.2	Flow chart at Shouldice Hospital	103

8.3	Leisure and business demand	107
8.4	Maximizing revenue	107
8.5	Average queue length	110
8.6	Control of variability	110
8.7	Waiting-line configurations	111
9.1	Value creation cycle for water distribution	114
9.2	Value creation cycle of an original equipment manufacturer	115
9.3	Value creation cycle for aftermarket users	116
9.4	Elements of the service proposition for the industrial aftermarket	117
9.5	Local customer support	118
9.6	The service triangle for professional services	119
9.7	Positioning consulting and accounting firms	120
9.8	Commoditization of consulting services	121
9.9	Positioning of stockbroking firms	124
9.10	Segmentation of Merrill Lynch customer base	125
9.11	The leaking bucket model	126
10.1	The dynamics of continuous improvement	128
10.2	Performance after initial impulsion	128
10.3	The diffusion model	133
10.4	Four factors at play in the conversion of attempts	135
10.5	Reconsidering the four factors at play	136
10.6	Consolidation factors	139

Tables

1.1	Evolution of employment by sector in the United States	10

INTRODUCTION

Today, more and more attention is paid to the service sector of the economy, whose rapid growth has led it to outstrip the two other sectors, agriculture and industry. Its dominance, the variety of services offered and the multiplicity of cross-functional management issues it raises have rendered the classic paradigm of a three-sector economy obsolete and misleading.

How is it possible to make sense of all this diversity and come up with an operational definition of services? The strength of a new definition lies in how far it is able to retain simplicity and economy while being powerful enough to explain and organize the existing concepts and approaches used to explore the field.

This book is an account of the definition of services based on the separation between back-stage and front-stage activities. Services deal with the front-stage interactions; production and manufacturing with the back-stage operations. The idea is very simple but goes against the traditional separation between management disciplines such as marketing, operations management, organizational behavior and human resources management. With this definition, we are all in services to a greater or lesser extent, as any business involves both front-stage interactions and back-stage operations. It is this "more or less" front-stage aspect that is highly rewarding to investigate, as long as its specificity is well understood.

This idea is simple but powerful. It will be shown that it is the best way to explore the variety of existing services – from industrial to professional – and the related management issues. It should become clearer why it is no longer possible to distinguish between the product and the process, why marketing, operations and people issues all merge in the front stage. It should become clearer why quality, productivity and flexibility issues are so specific in services.

The objective of the book is to prove that the proposed definition is robust enough to cover the whole business spectrum, and that the approach derived from it will provide a blueprint with which to explore all kinds of services and plan successful services strategy.

This back-stage/front-stage concept is obviously not new, but where this book breaks new ground is in using it to systematically explore all important issues of the field with a number of instruments, including the service mix, the service triangle and the service-intensity matrix.

This book is written not for readers who wish to deepen and refine their reflection in a precise domain, but for those who seek an overview of the very wide world of services, an orientation map with which to explore the terrain and their own experience, a method for positioning, designing and implementing any kind of service.

The book unfolds in a logical sequence. After reviewing traditional classifications, Chapter 1 introduces the new definition and helps the reader understand the extent to which we are all in services now. Chapter 2 establishes the distinction between the front and the back stage and outlines a key issue: how to align these two very different worlds. The next step is to unfold the new service approach – the service triangle – in Chapter 3. A number of important issues now become visible, from the need to develop a dual partnership culture to the importance of shedding light on quality gaps. The service-intensity matrix in Chapter 4 is a good instrument to position any type of service, as shown by a number of examples from different industries.

Chapter 5 focuses on the key issue of creating breakthrough services by finding and keeping a good fit between the value perceived by the different stakeholders and the service proposition.

Chapters 6 and 7 analyze the difference between quality of product and quality of service, and guide the reader to the three movements of quality.

Chapter 8 deals with another service-specific issue: balancing supply and demand. It is about time in Chapter 9 to show the value and usefulness of concepts and instruments developed so far and how they apply at the two ends of the service continuum. At one end, industrial services are still close to the product, and at the other, professional services focus on client interaction.

Finally, Chapter 10 considers how to manage the change process. As managers strive to re-create value with strategic repositioning, new service propositions or continuous improvement, they have to focus on implementation and put in place a systematic change process.

Throughout the book, a number of images, graphs and symbols should help readers assimilate and memorize the main ideas and concepts, using both sides of their brains. My objective was to keep the book as short as possible, as I know that managers do not have much time and prefer a picture to a thousand words.

This book has greatly benefited from questions, discussions and contributions from participants in seminars at INSEAD, and in companies too numerous to list here. I would like to thank Stephen Chick, Christoph Loch, Ben Bensaou, Jens Meyer and Yves Doz for their numerous suggestions and improvements, Lillian Haas for her editorial assistance, and Claire Derouin for her patience in typing and retyping the manuscript. Finally, this work could not have been completed without the help of INSEAD.

Inevitably, in writing this book I have borrowed a lot, and it is impossible to quote all sources, although I have tried to give the main ones in the text. The rest are in the bibliography. For myself and, I hope, for the reader, what is important is the journey itself. While writing this book, certain issues became clearer to me, and it is this new clarity of thought, expressed in the front-stage/back-stage concept, that I want to share with you in the following chapters. The only originality I would claim is the demonstration that the definition of services is robust enough to travel over the whole field of services, and to address the main issues from a proper perspective.

1

TOWARD A NEW DEFINITION OF SERVICES

The service sector is the dominant part of the economy, and yet its exact nature is poorly defined.

Most people will agree with the British magazine *The Economist* that a service is "anything sold in trade that cannot be dropped on your foot." They will also agree that this sector excludes harvesting the land or manufacturing automobiles. Differences of opinion rapidly surface, however, when we try to explain what exactly a service is, rather than what it is not. Any analysis is thus confronted with the complex issue of definition. What do all these activities that we call services have in common? What are their basic characteristics? What lessons can be drawn from a new definition?

THE CLASSIC THREE-SECTOR CLASSIFICATION

One approach to defining services involves first ruling out all activities we know are not services. This approach leads to the tripartite classification of the sectors of the economy. From this traditional viewpoint, services represent the tertiary sector: the third part of the trinity completed by agriculture (the primary sector) and manufacturing (the industrial sector). Let us examine whether this first definition is satisfactory.

According to the three-sector model, economic development followed a natural three-phase sequence. At first, agriculture dominated in terms of output and exchange and, due to its low productivity, employed most members of society. This was followed by the industrial (or secondary) sector, which developed rapidly and brought significant improvements in productivity, due mainly to economies of scale. This development permitted the blooming of the service (or tertiary) sector, which used the freed workforce. This final sector then rapidly expanded to become in time the largest of the three.

4

In the United States by 2002, 76 percent of the working population was employed in services, leaving only 2.6 percent in agriculture (see Figure 1.1).

The shift in employment from farming to the other two sectors is one of the most remarkable changes seen in the last century and has been noted all over the world.

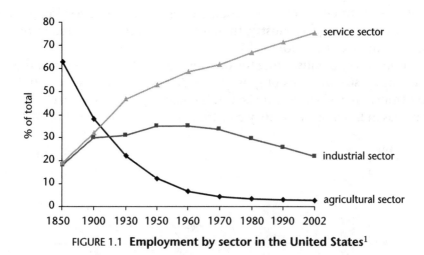

FIGURE 1.1 **Employment by sector in the United States[1]**

At the beginning of the 20th century in Japan, almost 70 percent of the labor force worked in farming, compared with 40 percent in the United States and only 20 percent in Great Britain. In 2002, these figures were 5.3 percent for Japan, 2.6 percent for the United States and 1.8 percent for Great Britain.

It is worth noting that over the past 30 years, a similarly significant fall in employment has been seen in the manufacturing sector. Though clearly less linear, this evolution is no less interesting. According to British economists Richard Brown and Julius DeAnne,[2] farming and manufacturing went through a similar evolution:

Both exhibit rising productivity through labor-saving technological change. Both produce easily tradable output so that incremental productive capacity can migrate to low-cost locations.

According to these authors, we can therefore expect that:

1. Manufacturing employment will continue to fall in OECD countries, dropping to levels of 10 percent or below over the next 30 years.
2. Those countries where manufacturing employment is currently highest – Germany and Japan – will see a more rapid decrease in employment.

If recent structural changes in employment have not resulted in a shift from farming to industry, then jobs have been transferred principally to the service sector.

Another way of illustrating the development of the service sector is to measure its size in terms of gross domestic product (see Figure 1.2). In the United States, services make up the majority of the country's GDP, whereas in India or China they constitute less than 50 percent of GDP.

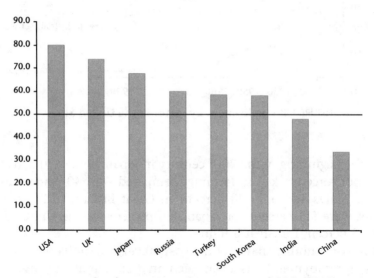

FIGURE 1.2 **Service sector as a percentage of GDP (2003)**

We now understand something of the importance of the service sector in our economies, but it is interesting to note that serious analysis of the actual content of this sector and its impact has started only recently.

One reason is the reluctance to deal with nondurable goods or to delve into an area commonly associated with servitude. This perception is deeply rooted in the history of economics and is observed among followers of both Adam Smith and Karl Marx. Adam Smith wrote in his book, *The Wealth of Nations*, published in 1776:

> The labor of some of the most respectable orders in society is like that of menial servants, *unproductive of any value*, and does not fix or realize itself in any vendible commodity which endures after that labor is past. In the same class must be ranked some both of the gravest and most important, and some of the most frivolous professions: churchmen, lawyers, physicians, men of letters, players, buffoons, musicians, opera-singers, and so on.

This quotation reveals a certain contempt for the service sector. It was considered unproductive and transient, and churchmen were mixed with buffoons.

This attitude was unfortunately upheld throughout the 20th century. The contempt for services shown by theoreticians of centralized planning played a large part in leaving this sector underdeveloped in the economies of Eastern Europe, Russia and China. Consequently, these countries had, and continue to have, great difficulty transporting, distributing, financing, processing and maintaining the goods they produce. Even today, the view that manufacturing jobs require more skills than services remains widespread, and service workers are still frequently caricatured as "hamburger-flippers" or "public entertainers."

But the more we consider the service sector, the more we discover that it is clearly too vast and ill-defined to serve as a definition. It actually represents the rest of the economy. It is too broad and includes too many different economic activities. At the heart of this sector policemen and prostitutes, bankers and truck drivers, schoolteachers and hairdressers all rub shoulders. It should not, however, be rejected immediately. Perhaps a classification carried out inside the service sector would allow us to visualize it more accurately.

A MORE DETAILED CLASSIFICATION

The Browning-Singlemann classification describes the different economic sectors as follows (Figure 1.3):

- Extractive (agriculture, mining)
- Transformative (construction, food, manufacturing): second sector

- Producer services (business services and marketed services)
- Personal services (domestic, hotel, repair, dry-cleaning, entertainment, and so on)
- Distributive services (logistics, communication, wholesale and retail trade)
- Nonmarketed services (health, welfare, government, and so on)

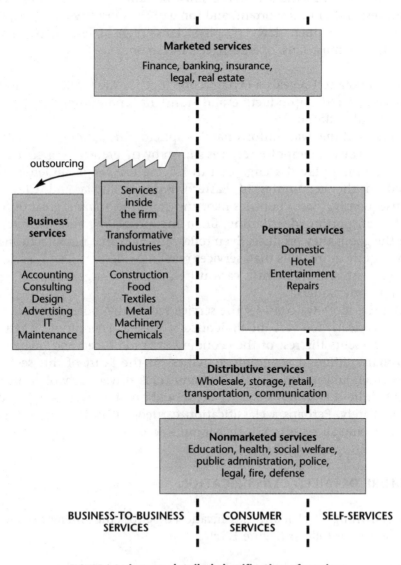

FIGURE 1.3 **A more detailed classification of services**

The whole picture can be broken down vertically into another three-sector classification:

- business-to-business services
- consumer services
- and self-services

according to their proximity to the final customer.

Business-to-business services

Companies have always used services provided by other firms, such as distribution, financing and insurance. In recent years, however, the demand for producer services increased considerably as these companies began outsourcing tasks they used to deal with internally, such as data processing, legal advice, advertising, design, research, cleaning and security. The principal aims were to reduce costs and improve labor force flexibility, but also to increase specialization, as the service provider had more specific experience and expertise than the producer.

The jobs outsourced in this way cannot be considered new positions, but simply a shift in employment from manufacturing to services. Through this outsourcing process, an increasing number of so-called manufacturing jobs are moving to independent structures defined in national accounts as services.

Consumer services

These are either marketed services (including banking and insurance services that are sold directly to consumers for their personal use) or traditionally nonmarketed services, such as health and education. While government policies have expanded social welfare and certain local services, the growth of marketed consumer services on the whole has been more sluggish.

Self-services

When consumers provide required services for themselves, this is defined as self-service, and there is general agreement that this is one way to increase productivity. So maids and other servants, barbers and live entertainment have all, to a greater or lesser extent, been replaced by washing machines, vacuum cleaners, dishwashers, electric razors and televisions.

Overall evolution

Let us now return to the overall evolution of the different sectors and subsectors in the United States, as shown in Table 1.1 (we would expect similar evolution in other developed countries).

TABLE 1.1 **Evolution of employment by sector in the United States**

	1970 78.36 million %	1980 99.32 million %	1990 116.03 million %	2002 129.93 million %
AGRICULTURE – subtotal	4.42	3.38	2.78	2.57
INDUSTRY SECTOR – subtotal	33.29	29.34	25.73	21.81
Mining	0.66	0.99	0.64	0.40
Construction	6.15	6.26	6.69	7.44
Manufacturing	26.48	22.09	18.40	13.97
SERVICES SECTOR – subtotal	62.29	67.28	71.49	75.62
Producer services	6.83	9.92	13.39	14.30
Finance, insurance and real estate	5.04	6.04	6.94	7.03
Business services	1.79	3.88	6.46	7.27
Personal services	7.66	7.55	6.52	5.33
Distributive services	26.95	26.91	28.26	29.08
Transport and communication	6.79	6.57	7.04	7.45
Wholesale and retail trade	20.16	20.34	21.22	21.63
Nonmarketed services	20.85	22.90	23.32	26.91
Government	5.72	5.38	4.85	4.76
Hospitals and health services	5.70	7.43	8.05	9.74
Primary and secondary schools	7.82	5.59	5.16	6.21
Higher education		2.11	2.28	2.34
Social services	1.06	1.60	1.93	2.76
Legal services	0.55	0.79	1.05	1.10
Total	**100.00**	**100.00**	**100.00**	**100.00**

Source: *United States Statistical Abstracts, 2003*

As noted earlier, farming and manufacturing are in decline. Within the tertiary sector, nonmarketed services and distribution take pride of place, but the most striking evolution is without doubt that of producer services. This growth is largely due to the gradual increase in importance of business services.

Finally, if we consider the development of employment in the service sector over the next few years, we can expect a stabilization in personal services, an increase in nonmarketed services (largely due to growth in health services) and a significant extension in producer services. The fastest growth rate will be for knowledge workers and professionals, whereas the highest growth in the number of jobs will involve the least-qualified positions. Most of these new jobs will offer little in the way of career prospects. It is likely that fast-food employees, office workers, cleaners, waiters and drivers, among others, will be employed permanently in this way, with few prospects for career progression.

LIMITS OF THESE CLASSIFICATIONS

It is clear that services are neither agriculture nor industry. They are what is left, the complement. However, the improved classification does not provide greater understanding of the specificity of services; we simply have more homogeneous categories of activities.

The artificial nature of the distinction between the industry and the service sectors

The distinction between industry and service sectors is, in fact, largely irrelevant. Clearly, these two sectors are evolving in symbiosis: services cannot prosper without a powerful industrial sector, and industry is dependent on services.

Products can be seen as the physical embodiment of the service provided: cars provide comfortable transport, and television sets deliver entertainment.

This inevitably means that in today's world, the distinction between industry and services becomes artificial and meaningless. Although an elevator manufacturer usually also provides maintenance services, its activity as a whole is classified as manufacturing. Yet if a separate firm specifically performs these same maintenance activities, it falls into the services category. Financial and insurance services are one of General Motors' main "products."

And just as manufacturers are moving toward services, so service providers tend to "industrialize" their activities, as the evolution of McDonald's restaurants shows. However, there are clear limits to how far this trend can go, given the lack of flexibility and increased impersonality associated with industrialization.

Dividing economic activities into three or more sectors is therefore futile and cannot lead to a clear and operational definition of services. We should adopt the opposite approach, by first defining what we mean by service and then seeing if this definition is useful and operational.

"PURE" SERVICES

Probably the best way to understand the difference between services and manufacturing is to contrast the two activities using a black-box approach to represent each – and asking the simple questions "What goes into the black box?" and "What comes out?"

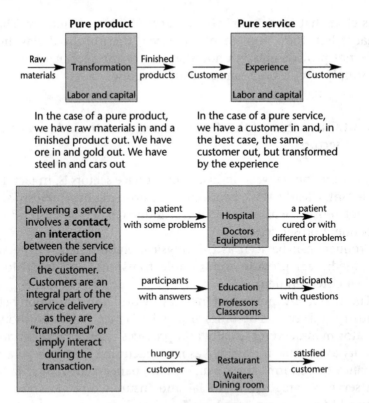

FIGURE 1.4 **A black-box approach**

The service provider's actions directly affect the customer. This experience is essentially *intangible*, even though it may include tangible elements such as manufactured goods, meals or information.

A hotel room should have a positive effect on a traveler's comfort, and legal advice should have a beneficial impact on the potential liability of a lawyer's client.

A product is an object, a device, a thing, whereas a service is an act, a unique performance. Although the provision of most services is supported by tangible elements, the essence of what is bought is a performance given by one party for another.

This interaction generally takes place in what we call the front stage. Depending on the type of service provided, the level of contact may be fairly high or intensive, as an experience in a gourmet restaurant, or brief and sporadic, as a simple banking transaction. Even less-intensive contacts may take place by telephone or online.

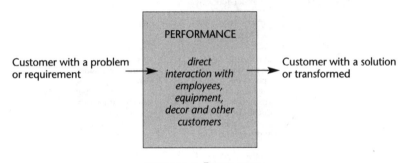

FIGURE 1.5 **Front stage**

Let us now contrast the service experience with the manufacturing of products: here, entering the black box are raw materials or information. The output is a finished product or processed information. These activities take place inside the "factory," more generally what we call the back stage, away from the customer's presence, as shown in Figure 1.6.

Pure services and pure products are extreme cases. In actual fact, whether a service is delivered or a product manufactured, both the front and the back stages are involved. It is their relative importance that will determine whether the activity is predominantly service or product (see Figure 1.7). This means that we are all in services, more or less.

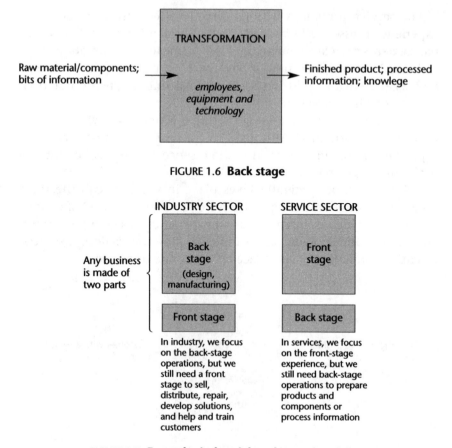

FIGURE 1.6 **Back stage**

FIGURE 1.7 **From the industrial to the service sector**

What is important is the difference between front stage and back stage – two very different worlds – and not the traditional distinction between the industry and the service sectors.

WE ARE ALL IN SERVICES NOW, MORE OR LESS

This idea that any manufacturing or service delivery involves activities in both the front stage and the back stage was expressed by Theodore Levitt as early as 1972:[3]

There are no such things as service industries. There are only industries whose service components are greater or lesser than those of other industries. Everybody is in service.

Levitt's idea was not developed further, and his message was lost. The objective of this book is to show that this message leads naturally to the definition of services as front-stage activities. Restaurants, for example, are all in services, more or less. The service part of a restaurant is the dining room, and the production part is the kitchen.

The "more or less" aspect appears clearly in a comparison of the dining rooms of a McDonald's and a gourmet restaurant (see Figure 1.8).

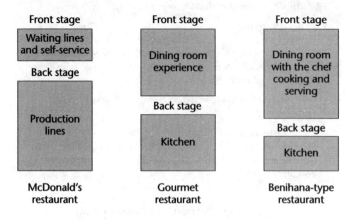

FIGURE 1.8 **Three types of restaurant**

The service component of the gourmet restaurant – the dining room – is much more developed than the front stage of the McDonald's, which consists of waiting lines and a self-service room. On the other hand, in the back stage of the McDonald's, production lines manufacture standard products like hamburgers. Industrializing services means simplifying the front stage and focusing on the product in the back stage to achieve productivity and economies of scale.

If the chef moves from the back stage to the front, the service experience is enriched by his presence; he will cook, serve, interact and deliver a show. This is the service concept of the Benihana of Tokyo restaurants. The service aspect is clearly enhanced.

The same approach applies to activities dealing with information or knowledge. According to our definition, production must include the processing of information as well as the processing of raw materials.

Information is just another type of raw material, one with specific properties (see Figure 1.9). A software program is a product. On the other hand, in the front stage, the service aspect is about distribution, adaptation, learning, consulting or training. Products and information are used to enrich the relationship with the customer.

Data and any sort of information should be considered as raw materials.

They are laboriously manipulated, stored and transformed when their support is physical (paper, books, etc.).

With the digitization revolution, information is:

- **easily processed**
  Words, voice, music, data, films, files and pictures are turned into bits that can easily be modified, shaped, chopped up, crunched, downloaded, uploaded, edited at high speed. Hence the notion of databank, data warehousing, data mining, data consolidation.

- **easily customized, enriched, accumulated, transformed into knowledge**

- **easily distributed**
  Bits of information are easily and speedily spread and disseminated (infinite scalability and reach), hence the difficulty of ownership and protection.

FIGURE 1.9 **Properties of information**

WE SHALL BE MORE AND MORE IN SERVICES IN THE FUTURE

Examples from the industrial sector, such as the supplier of braking systems for auto assemblers[4] in Figure 1.10, show the expansion of the service aspect of most businesses. A firm that was mainly focused on back-stage operations had to develop its front end under pressure from customers to provide more customized solutions and better interaction.

The back-stage organization that was focused on product excellence and economies of scale in three regions had simple front-end structures to link to markets and customers with liaison engineers, sales and marketing.

The new structure in Figure 1.11 shows the increased size of the front stage to better serve global markets and large customers with business and program managers. According to the new definition, the company has increased the service aspect of its activity.

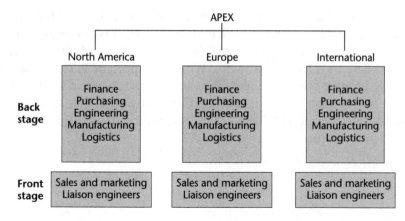

FIGURE 1.10 **Previous organizational structure**

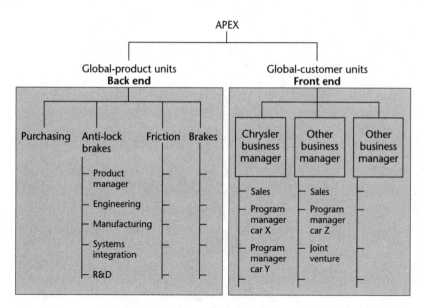

FIGURE 1.11 **New organizational structure**

CONCLUSION

As front end and back end become more differentiated, the next challenge is to align and coordinate them, despite the inherent conflict between the product logic and the customer relationship approach.

We are all in services now, more or less, but we will be even more in services in the future as the back end shrinks with economies of scale and outsourcing and the front end develops further with more sophisticated demands from customers. What is important is to weigh the relative importance of the back stage and the front stage and to understand how to manage these two very different worlds that are often in conflict but need to be aligned and coordinated. This is the objective of the next chapters.

2

SERVICES: THE FRONT-STAGE EXPERIENCE

Attempts to isolate the three sectors of the economy are highly artificial. Any activity should be considered as a composite of front-stage and back-stage elements – the dining room of a restaurant and the kitchen. The customer experiences the service in the front stage. The back stage is the "product zone," where a physical transformation takes place.

At the counter of a bank, the clerk answers inquiries or carries out financial transactions in direct contact with customers. When the services cannot be provided immediately, the customer's request becomes a paper record or a computer file, which is handed over to the back stage. The information is then processed factory-style, passing from one workstation to another with intermediate storage.

On a flight from Paris to New York, passengers travel inside the actual transport-producing instrument: they are consuming travel at exactly the same time as the airline is producing it, and the idea of any time lag between production and consumption is nonsense. Since the passenger is directly involved in the production process before, during and after the journey, many interactions may take place, ranging from visiting a travel agency, to making telephone reservations and checking in, to talking to the air stewards, to collecting baggage. Each of these contacts is a "moment of truth."[1] We should also note that both in the airport and on board the plane, the passenger will be only vaguely aware of the support systems in the background: baggage handling, aircraft maintenance, air traffic control, preparation of meals, and so on.

Every activity, therefore, consists of both an interaction (the service aspect) and a material transformation (the product aspect). It is the respective weight of these two elements that makes the service aspect more or less pronounced. This distinction is essential because, as will become clear later, managing a direct interaction is very different from managing a transformation, physical or informational.

19

As the new definition of service is based on the fundamental distinction between front and back stage, it is useful to check its validity by reviewing different activity sectors (see Figure 2.1).

IDENTIFYING THE SERVICE COMPONENT

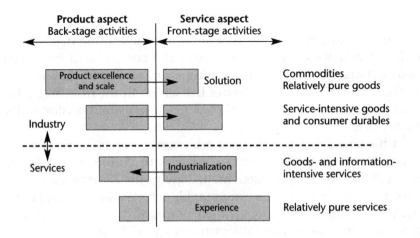

FIGURE 2.1 **The importance of the service component according to economic sector**

The first category to be considered is relatively *"pure" goods* or commodities. This includes primary products such as steel; paper; glass; aluminum; agricultural and chemical products; and packaged goods such as food, soap and toothpaste, sold in supermarkets or vending machines. The interactive part of the service (mainly sales and marketing) is quite limited, and price becomes the dominant factor in these simple transactions.

For a supplier of gas such as Air Liquide or Air Products, the price is the main differentiator, as one molecule of gas is identical to another molecule of gas. So when the focus is on the product, a natural strategy to become number one or number two in the industry is to get low cost through economies of scale and mass production.

Another approach is to focus on the customer and sell a solution, not just a product. This means understanding how the customer creates value and providing him with adequate products and services at each stage of his value creation cycle. For example, if the customer is a fish farmer, Air Liquide may provide a variety of services around products and equipment, as shown in Figure 2.2.

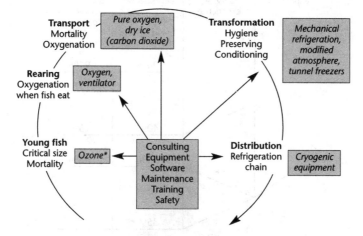

* Ozone's very strong oxidation properties are sufficient to kill microorganisms in water treatment

FIGURE 2.2 **Value creation cycle of a fish farmer**

The next category is *consumer durables* such as automobiles, electric appliances and computers. Services are essential for this category, both to develop the relationship with customers (by providing specific services such as an intelligible user guide or telephone advice) and for maintenance of the product. Where sophisticated equipment and machines such as robots are involved, a special relationship with the buyer and subsequent users is required, as is the development of specific services in terms of logistics, distribution and maintenance. This relationship may evolve toward a long-term partnership.

When a bank buys 500 PCs, it buys products and related services. When it buys a consumer banking system, it buys a system that works, not a collection of products. As a result, the supplier does the systems integration (consulting, application software and customer education), which becomes a front-end function. The supplier does part of the client's job by increasing its presence.

Let's now consider car distribution and focus on two successive aspects (see Figure 2.3): the sales experience (the satisfaction with the car bought) and the after-sales service experience.

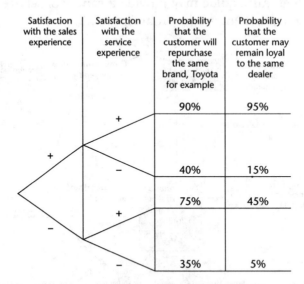

Satisfaction with the sales experience	Satisfaction with the service experience	Probability that the customer will repurchase the same brand, Toyota for example	Probability that the customer may remain loyal to the same dealer
	+	90%	95%
+			
	−	40%	15%
		75%	45%
	+		
−			
	−	35%	5%

FIGURE 2.3 **Performance leads, but service wins**

In this case, even if Toyota provides a good car, it may lose the loyalty of its customers if the dealer does a bad job. On the other hand, the dealer may help Toyota recover if the customer is not happy with the car. This diagram shows clearly the importance of the service aspect of the business, and we may say, using a well-known motto: "Performance leads, but service wins."

Below the dotted line separating the industrial sector from the service sector (Figure 2.1) are two further categories: *goods- and information-intensive services* (such as restaurants, hotels and banks) and *relatively pure services* (such as hairdressing and legal advice).

Let's consider the first category. Two important considerations when choosing a bank are often the value of the advice given and the quality of the relationship offered by the account manager in the branch. However, customers may not be willing to pay a great deal or travel a long distance for a standard, basic transaction.

Thus, some goods- or information-intensive services can offer better prospects of productivity improvement if the interaction can be simplified (by replacing face-to-face contact with a machine or online contact, for example) and if economies of scale in the back stage can be achieved through bulk processing. This explains the growth in call centers and online businesses. To cut costs and achieve economies of scale, the interface is reduced to a minimum, and the activities are shifted to the back stage. The trend now is to industrialize services.

Relatively pure services (such as hairdressing, law firms, consulting and entertainment) are labor-intensive and offer few prospects of productivity gains, since it is difficult to reduce the contact time.

In conclusion, the dotted line separating the service sector from the industrial sector is less significant than the solid line dividing back-stage and front-stage activities, products and services.

We are all in services now, more or less.

This is in line with Baumol's service categories:[2]

- *Stagnant services* (health, education, personal services), in which productivity gains are difficult to achieve because quality is highly correlated with time spent in contact with the customer. In these sectors, new technologies may improve the quality of the service, but not the productivity.
- *Progressive services* (communication services), where customer-producer contact can be reduced and standardized, permitting high productivity growth and strong penetration of advanced technologies.
- *Asymptotically stagnant services* (television, radio and computer services), in which productivity, after spectacular growth in the early stages of development through the automation of support and back-stage activities, diminishes as the volume of labor-intensive interactions increases.

FRONT STAGE AND BACK STAGE: TWO DIFFERENT WORLDS

To demonstrate the value of our service definition, we contrast front-stage and back-stage activities.

Product excellence and scale in the back stage

The mass production of the industrial revolution is based on two basic concepts: *division of labor*, or specialization, and *standardization*. The result of the transformation of raw materials into finished products or of the processing of information is tangible, measurable and specific, even if it is a matter of electronic bits.

Stocks of raw materials, work in progress and finished goods are the result of division of labor and imbalances between capacity and demand. Stocks are a useful buffer to level off production even in the age of stockless and just-in-time operations.

The essence of standardization is to define clear limits, or tolerances, for the characteristics of products. Processes and products are controlled according to these specifications at all stages of the transformation, from inspection of raw materials to final test. The final objective is zero defects – that is, no product outside specified tolerances. This can be achieved only by reducing the spread and the standard deviation as much as possible. Variation is the enemy.

When a defect occurs, the product is reworked, but this operation remains invisible to the customer. With specialization and mass production, larger and larger production sites are built. Production gets centralized in factories situated at quite a distance from the final customer.

Solutions and customer experience in the front stage

Services are essentially *intangible*, as they are produced and consumed simultaneously. They cannot be displayed, owned and bought in the same way as a product. Nor can they be protected by filing a patent. To demonstrate a service, it is often necessary to provide a sample.

One way to make the interaction more tangible is to transform it into a memorable, distinctive experience. A trip to the grocery store can become an exciting event if music, exotic scenery and lighting create a theatrical shopping environment.

Having the customer inside the delivery system creates a major source of uncertainty, since employees must interact directly with people whose behavior cannot be predicted with any degree of consistency. Customers, far from being passive, are a highly reactive "raw material" that is particularly difficult to control. They may change their minds over time or even while the service is being performed. The different terms used to describe customers illustrate the great variety of roles they may play: user, subscriber, beneficiary, spectator, taxpayer, number, patient, guest, visitor. This makes standardization very difficult, if not impossible. Each customer is unique; each encounter is unique.

Now, what about division of labor and specialization? This is not welcomed by customers, who certainly prefer to deal with the same employee for the whole interaction. They want to deal with the same bank officer and certainly do not want to queue at different counters to complete a transaction. They would avoid dealing with different lawyers for different aspects of the same transaction. They want one-stop shopping, seamless interaction – *integration.*

Customers are an integral part of the performance and therefore have an important role to play. This role may be purely routine or may require a specific effort, such as providing information to help a medical diagnosis or taking part in the search for a solution. Customers guide and control the service provider and can even be involved before or after the contact, as is the case with students, for example, who prepare for classes beforehand and do homework afterward. So, far from being "objects" subject to a process of blind transformation, customers can help improve the design of the service and the way in which it is delivered. Although the *participation* of customers is a source of uncertainty, it is also vital for any improvement in the effectiveness of the service provided. In this sense, customers can be considered as part-time employees, or *co-producers.*

Because a service is a performance, it can be neither owned nor accumulated but must be consumed at the moment of production. Outside the delivery process, it has no existence. Services, therefore, cannot be stored in inventory or hoarded. It is clearly impossible to possess a theater performance or last week's flight to Rome. Unconsumed services are lost for good. When demand exceeds capacity, the customer is either "stored" (by having to wait in line) or lost. When capacity exceeds demand, some of the capacity will remain unused (empty hospital beds, vacant hotel rooms or excess staff, for example). It is therefore vital to adjust supply to fit the demand and to maximize the use of capacity.

Because a service is a one-off performance in the presence of the customer, it has to be *right the first time*, at the very moment of delivery. Contrary to what happens in a factory, once a service has been delivered it is difficult to improve or correct it. The performance cannot be measured, controlled or corrected during the delivery without the customer's being aware of it.

It is also much more difficult to find out how the customer perceives the experience during the interaction; the perception is immediate, subjective and qualitative. If something does go wrong during the delivery, the customer must be "repaired" or "recovered." So whereas in the back stage the objective is zero defects, in the front stage it is *zero defections*.

In fact, each "moment of truth" is made up of several interactions: with people, with other customers, with the delivery process.

Customers have a global evaluation of the service. Every time an element of the interaction is right, they credit their "satisfaction account." However, every time their experience fails to match their expectations, they debit this account. Unfortunately, one debit equals several credits, and a single minus or defect could ruin the whole experience.

As Jan Carlzon explained in *Moments of Truth*:[3]

Last year, each of our 10 million customers came in contact with approximately five Scandinavian Airlines employees, and this contact lasted an average of 15 seconds each time. Thus, Scandinavian Airlines is "created" in the minds of our customers 50 million times a year, 15 seconds at a time. These 50 million "moments of truth" are the moments that ultimately determine whether Scandinavian Airlines will succeed or fail as a company.

Because services are produced and consumed simultaneously, they have to be located near to customers. This is particularly true for hotels, restaurants and shops, where location is a key success factor. Services do not have distribution networks; they are produced and delivered through networks of decentralized units such as branches, agencies or chains of restaurants and stores. However, ease of access and convenient location play a less significant role when the physical presence of the customer is unnecessary, thanks to call centers or online communication.

From marketing and selling a product to marketing and selling an experience

The traditional marketing mix of the four P's (product, price, promotion and place) is essentially aimed at winning new customers. It relies on mass communications, with customers considered as statistical units in a targeted segment, rather than as individuals requiring personalized treatment.

According to Sandra Vandemerwe:[4]

> By and large, relationships between producers and consumers were mostly "transactional" in the 1960s, assigned to professional sales people who were expected to sell as much and as many "things" as possible. A more "relational" approach began to catch on in the 1970s when marketing began seeking a better understanding of markets and customers. In the late 1980s, observers were advocating so-called "interactive" relationships, specifically demanding stronger ongoing bonds between a company and its customers.

And it is more so nowadays, with concepts such as "one to one" marketing. In manufacturing, goods are mostly sold after their production or creation. In the case of services, this sequence is inverted: the service is sold before it is produced. Its promotion is therefore based on an intangible "product."

The service mix

One of the aims of marketing is to make consumers aware of the existence of a product, and another is to convince them to buy it. However, the traditional marketing mix used to promote tangible goods (the four P's) is clearly inadequate for services.

First, the *promotion* of tangible goods through the usual media is less effective for pure services than word of mouth based on customers' experience. Second, the *place* of delivery is also the production site. *Price* sensitivity is also quite different: as a rule, a buyer will more readily accept the price quoted for a physical product than for an intangible service. In the latter case, firms must start with end users and work backward to produce the value that customers seek. Finally, it should be remembered that the performance covers not only the *product* – that is, the expected outcome – but also the delivery process and the interaction with employees.

To take this fact into account, two new P's should be added to the marketing mix: *process* and *people* (employees and customers). This mix of six P's represents the service mix.

The role of marketing is not only to attract new customers, but also to turn existing customers into repeat buyers and, if possible, into enthusiastic supporters of the brand. In services, transactional marketing is readily supplanted by relational marketing.

The importance of customer relationships is often ignored or underestimated. Many bank employees, for example, mistakenly believe that their role is limited to selling products when, in fact, they sell a relationship, an experience. Above all, customers appreciate dealing with well-known systems and familiar faces. By reinforcing personal contacts and aligning themselves with specific customer needs, service firms can build powerful barriers to entry, and justify higher prices.

The service triangle

Marketing therefore becomes an integrated function: responsibility for the contact lies with employees, who therefore become part-time marketers. This encounter between customers and employees during the interaction is often shown on the service triangle (Figure 2.4): the firm is placed at the top of the triangle, and customers and employees are placed on an equal level. Employees deliver, control and market their services, and clients take part in the production process (co-production), control and maybe even market the service (by word of mouth). Process and people (employees and customers) are essential elements of the service delivery.

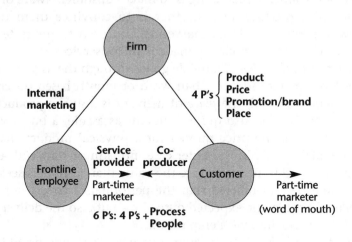

FIGURE 2.4 **The service triangle**

Clearly, the success of a service company depends on its ability to develop a satisfactory relationship with each of its customers and play with the service mix. By doing so, it will not only retain its customers – it will also sell them more services. It will thereby be able to increase revenues and reduce costs: either by means of what we call economies of scope – that is, by selling a wider range of services to the same customer (cross-selling) – or through economies of relationship when it is possible to reduce costs by regularly selling to the same customers.

Since employees play a vital part in promoting the service, it is essential that they fully understand their role and are willing to act as required. Before any external marketing takes place, it is therefore necessary to sell the service to those who are going to provide it; this calls for internal marketing. It is imperative that any communications campaign for a new service is targeted equally at employees (the internal customers) and external customers. The effort accorded to this internal marketing should be comparable with a manufacturer's attention to its distribution networks.

CONCLUSION

Comparing pure services in the front stage with pure products in the back stage has allowed us to see a number of differences (Figure 2.5):

Pure products in the back stage	Pure services in the front stage
Product excellence and scale	*Customer solutions and experience*
■ Tangible goods: ownership, patent	■ Intangible: no ownership, no patent
■ Division of labor and specialization	■ Integration: seamless experience
■ Standardization	■ Customization: each customer is unique
■ No participation of customer	■ Co-production
■ Scale	■ Scope, up-selling and cross-selling
■ Stocks and inventory management	■ Queues and capacity management
■ Quality of conformity	■ Quality of performance
	■ Moment of truth
■ Zero defects	■ Zero defections
■ Rework	■ Recovery
■ Centralization and production	■ Location close to customers
Marketing and selling a product	*Marketing and selling an experience*
■ Marketing mix: "4P"	■ Service mix: "6P" (2 extra P's: process and people)
■ Pricing based on cost	■ Pricing based on value
■ Transactional marketing	■ Relationship marketing
■ Control of channels of distribution	■ Internal marketing

FIGURE 2.5 **Comparing products to services**

The back stage and the front stage are clearly two different worlds. Lessons drawn from manufacturing do not necessarily apply to services, and vice versa. An insurance company can invest considerable amounts in its back-stage activities to achieve economies of scale, but this effort may lose much of its effectiveness if the company neglects its interface with customers.

However, understanding the difference between front stage and back stage does not mean that they must be separated. Our distinction, which is intentionally exaggerated, should not lead us to distort the reality. These two components are closely interwoven. They are both part of the same system, and back-stage activities exist to support the front stage.

A tight linkage between back and front end is necessary despite inherent conflicts and different priorities. Different solutions exist to align back stage and front stage.

The first solution is to ask customers to be more reasonable. Remember the Ford Model T: "Any color as long as it's black." But this approach is harder to realize as customers are increasingly demanding. In that case, the second solution is to ask the back stage to become more flexible. The back stage has to develop flexible production lines, flexible workshops or modular designs.

Another way to solve the conflict is to ask the same people to do both back and front activities by moving the back-stage operators to the front, as in the Benihana restaurants where the chef is moved from the kitchen to the dining room.

In any case, it may be beneficial to resort to integration mechanisms (coordination meetings or centers, marketing councils, and so on) or focus on key workflow processes linking back and front. Some flexibility can be introduced in the back stage by outsourcing noncore production activities. But when it comes to outsourcing or developing partnerships for front-stage activities, we should not forget Jack Welch's[5] cardinal rule of business: "Never allow anyone to get between you and your customers. Those relationships take too long to develop and are too valuable to lose."

It seems that we have in our hands a solid definition of services. It now remains to show in the next chapters how useful and operational this definition can be.

3

THE SERVICE TRIANGLE

The previous chapter illustrated the importance of understanding two types of business activity: back-stage activities that focus on the making of products, and front-stage activities that focus on service, the interaction between frontline personnel and customers. These two need to be aligned in spite of their differences.

FROM TRANSACTION TO RELATIONSHIP

If the focus is too much on product excellence and productivity, there is a risk of considering the front stage simply as a channel of distribution. This transactional approach is epitomized by the famous marketing mix depicted in Figure 3.1. Products are pushed through the channels or pulled by customers. As they are things, tangible and measurable, their price is mostly based on a "cost plus" calculation.

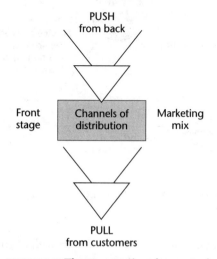

FIGURE 3.1 **The transactional approach**

In the service triangle, depicted in Figure 3.2, the transactional approach is represented by the direct link between the firm and the customer through product marketing, or between the customer and the frontline employee through sale, local marketing and promotion.

Internal marketing
• Channel selection
• Bundling of products
• Sales force support

Product marketing
• Product features
• Positioning and pricing
• Mass communication
• Brand

Firm

Transaction

Channel — Transaction through channel — Customer

Local sales and marketing
• Package pricing
• Promotion

FIGURE 3.2 **Marketing and selling a product**

When the focus is on services, the relationship between frontline staff and customers becomes predominant (see Figure 3.3).

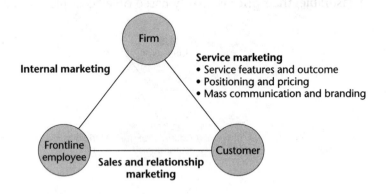

Firm

Internal marketing

Service marketing
• Service features and outcome
• Positioning and pricing
• Mass communication and branding

Frontline employee

Customer

Sales and relationship marketing

FIGURE 3.3 **Marketing and selling a service**

Frontline employees deliver the service as well as market it. The firm may blow its trumpet and assert value through mass communication, speeches, brochures or newsletters, but it is frontliners who demonstrate the real value of the service, advocating it, delivering it and making the experience unique and memorable.

In a business-to-business context, selling and buying simple products is usually performed by two gatekeepers: sales and purchasing, which act as proxies for their respective organizations. The communication between their different functions can be depicted as a "bow tie" relationship (see Figure 3.4).

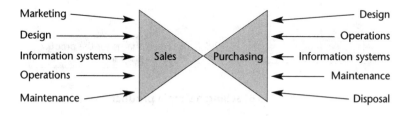

FIGURE 3.4 **"Bow tie" relationship**

Selling a simple product is finished when it is sold; selling a complex product or a service extends from the pre-sale to the after-sale experience. Many more people are involved before, during and after the purchasing decision. The interface between the two organizations gets wider and can be depicted as a "diamond" relationship (see Figure 3.5).

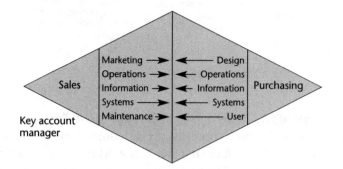

FIGURE 3.5 **Diamond relationship**

Selling a product and its related services in a business environment requires multiple interactions among many actors of both organizations from pre-sale to after-sale. Often an account manager called on by the selling organization has to analyze and integrate the relationship between his own team and the buyer's decision-making unit. He has to understand the role of different players: the initiator of the demand, the supporter, the gatekeeper, the influencer, the actual decision maker, the specifier, the buyer, the user. The service aspect on the front stage has to be extended.

This evolution from transaction to relationship can be represented by the following sequence:

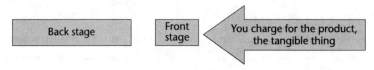

FIGURE 3.6 **Selling a simple product**

In the marketing mix, the product speaks for itself.

If the expected outcome of a service transaction is well established, as is the case with maintenance operations, travel or financial transactions, for example, the focus shifts to the tangible and measurable elements of the service mix: time spent, level of expertise required, intensity of interaction, documentation and explanations.

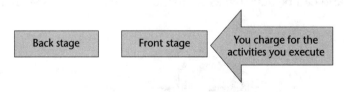

FIGURE 3.7 **Service transaction**

The old story of the boilermaker[1] illustrates the difference between charging for activities and charging for outcome. A boilermaker was hired to fix a steamship boiler that was not working well. After listening to the engineers and asking a few questions, he went to the boiler room. He looked at the maze of pipes, listened to the noise of the boiler and the hiss of escaping steam, and felt some pipes with his hand. Then he reached into his overalls, took out a small hammer and tapped a red valve. Immediately, the entire system began working perfectly, and the boilermaker went home.

When the steamship owner received a bill for $1,000, he complained that the boilermaker had been in the engine room for only fifteen minutes and requested a detailed bill. This is what the boilermaker sent to him:

For tapping with hammer $ 1
For knowing where to tap $ 999
$ 1,000

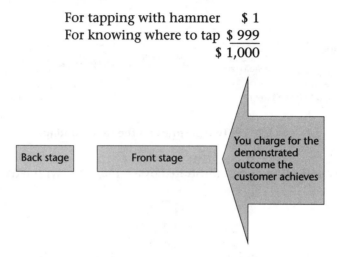

FIGURE 3.8 **Experience, transformation of client**

Likewise, a consultant should focus on the transformation of his client, on results and implementation, and spend less time on voluminous analytical documents or sophisticated PowerPoint presentations. Lawyers' "no win, no fee" policy says the same thing: what is important is the result, the outcome, the perceived value.

A DUAL-PARTNERSHIP CULTURE

Managing the relationship means dealing with a dual-partnership culture; the two partners are the frontline staff on one side and customers on the other side. At the Ritz-Carlton Hotel, ladies and gentlemen serve ladies and gentlemen.

Both constituencies are on the same footing. Employees should be considered as customers and customers as employees. A motto like "Do for your employees what you do for your customers" recognizes that both are part of the process of delivering value. Both have human needs that require attention.

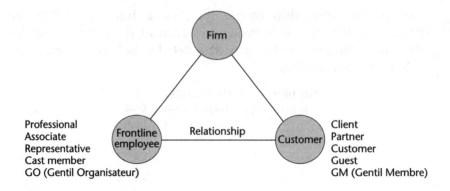

FIGURE 3.9 **Two partners on the same footing**

This dual culture is best illustrated by a remarkable symmetry of roles:

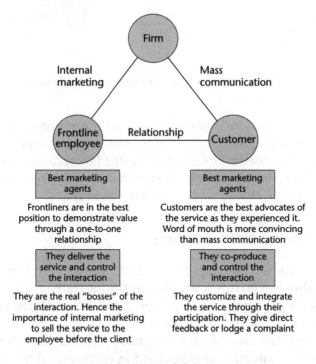

FIGURE 3.10 **Marketing and delivery symmetry**

As it is impossible to target and serve each customer individually, co-production allows customers to serve themselves in their own way, at their own pace, according to their own tastes. Customers are willing to pay for being employed by the firm because they get a customized and integrated service. They expect systems that respond fast and give them wide access to information or knowledge.

eBay is a good example of customer control of the interaction. Every eBay user has a feedback profile made up of comments from other users after a sale or a purchase. Each customer is under pressure from other customers to behave – the pressure of their peers.

This symmetry can be extended to management style and in particular to hiring, training and retention.

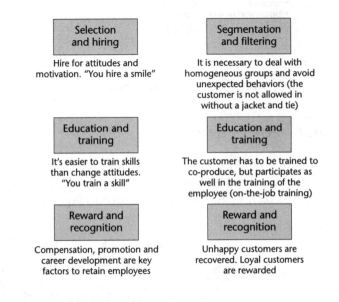

Selection and hiring	Segmentation and filtering
Hire for attitudes and motivation. "You hire a smile"	It is necessary to deal with homogeneous groups and avoid unexpected behaviors (the customer is not allowed in without a jacket and tie)
Education and training	Education and training
It's easier to train skills than change attitudes. "You train a skill"	The customer has to be trained to co-produce, but participates as well in the training of the employee (on-the-job training)
Reward and recognition	Reward and recognition
Compensation, promotion and career development are key factors to retain employees	Unhappy customers are recovered. Loyal customers are rewarded

FIGURE 3.11 **Extending the symmetry**

TURNING THE PYRAMID UPSIDE DOWN

The frontline staff deliver the service. They have a large portion of the control of the relationship in the front stage. Like players on a football field, they control the game; the coach is on the side during the game or in the back stage during training.

To recognize that the power is in the hands of the front-stage players, the traditional hierarchical pyramid should be turned upside down. Obviously, managers still have to give objectives and deal with accountability, but they have to become coaches. They have to empower and enable as well as guide, support, encourage and reward their frontline reports.

FIGURE 3.12 **Dual roles of managers**

THE SERVICE–PROFIT CHAIN

The service–profit chain establishes the link between profitability, customer satisfaction and employee satisfaction. This concept, developed by James Heskett et al.,[2] is best explained in Figure 3.13.

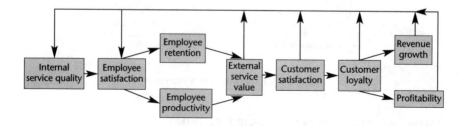

FIGURE 3.13 **The service–profit chain**

Good management and internal support lead to employee satisfaction which is essential to bring customer loyalty and profits. This linear chain can be nicely reorganized on the service triangle to reconnect the three elements: the firm, the customer and the employee. The dynamics of the service triangle are set in motion.

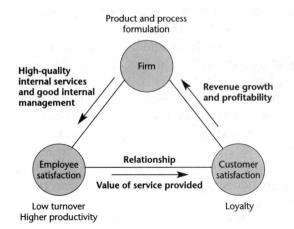

FIGURE 3.14 **The service–profit triangle**

The service–profit chain enhances the dual-partnership culture, as it is based on employee and customer satisfaction. It unfolds in this way:

- High-quality internal services and good internal management strongly influence employee satisfaction and thus the level of employee turnover and retention.
- Internal services relate to workplace design, selection and development of employees, management style, policies and procedures, information systems, internal communication, and rewards and recognition.
- The real cost of employee turnover, beyond hiring and retraining, is the loss of productivity and decreased customer satisfaction because the relationship has been interrupted.
- Employee satisfaction naturally drives customer satisfaction.
- Customer satisfaction in turn means revenue growth and profitability through increased loyalty (stream of revenues over time and cross-selling) and referrals. Word of mouth is particularly effective in a business-to-business environment.

POWER PLAY ON THE SERVICE TRIANGLE

If "products," methods and policies are designed and imposed from the top down, there is a risk that employees will feel boxed in and lack commitment. They are the real "bosses" of the moments of truth, and they have some freedom of action when it comes to selling a specific product or showing a definite attitude. They should be involved in creating and updating – if not the product, at least the process and procedures, as they have the final responsibility for customer satisfaction.

The more professional a service becomes, the more difficult it is for the organization to impose uniform norms and rules, as the firm must rely on the skills and know-how of its professionals.

But there is also a distinct possibility that, as employees become more autonomous, they may take advantage of their competence to gain even more independence and exert their own power on management and clients.

For their part, customers have some power over the relationship, as they decide whether or not to purchase (or repurchase) or advocate the service. It is well established, for example, that patients are more satisfied when they have reasonable control over their treatment than when doctors are in total control.

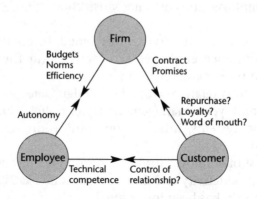

FIGURE 3.15 **Power play of the service triangle**

CONCLUSION

We are all in services, more or less. The more the focus is on the service aspect the more the transaction turns into a relationship, and the more the marketing mix moves the service mix.

In this dual-partnership culture, employees and customers play symmetrical roles.

THE SERVICE-INTENSITY MATRIX

The service mix combines "product" on one hand and process and people on the other – outcome and interaction, two natural dimensions that can be associated on two sides of the service-intensity matrix.

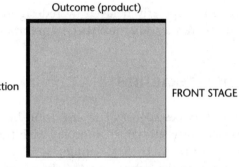

Outcome (product)

Intensity of interaction
(process, people)

FRONT STAGE

FIGURE 4.1 **The service-intensity matrix**

PRODUCT/OUTCOME DIMENSION

When buying a service, the customer is first and foremost looking at the outcome – the "product" dimension.

It is well known that over its life cycle, a new product is doomed to become mature and to shift toward normality and banality. When first launched the product is unique, customized and special, but it becomes standard and ordinary as it is mass-produced. Steve Jobs built his first personal computer in a garage, but now a computer is a commodity. A new and successful financial service is rapidly copied by competition and soon becomes commonplace.

This passage is the first axis, the "product" axis of the matrix. At one end, the offer is unique and highly customized and varied. At the other end, the service is routine and well understood by customers; it has become a standard. Specific and niche businesses are turned into vanilla commodity businesses. Commoditization is the fate of most activities, unless they are regenerated and re-created.

Product/outcome dimension

Varied, customized,
extended service or solution
(e.g. a complex financial transaction)

Limited and standard
service or solution
(e.g. a simple loan)

FIGURE 4.2 **Product dimension**

This shift can be regularly delayed by redesigning the offer. Hotels are regularly redecorated and refurbished to maintain their positioning.

INTENSITY OF INTERACTION

In high-contact services such as law firms and hospitals, the interaction is intense as many specialists interplay with the client, who often cooperates. By contrast, in low-contact services such as fast-food outlets and retail banks, employee involvement is rather low and customers know what they are expected to do.

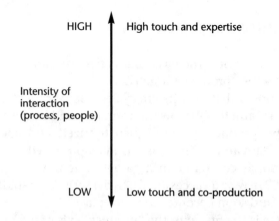

HIGH — High touch and expertise

Intensity of
interaction
(process, people)

LOW — Low touch and co-production

FIGURE 4.3 **Intensity of interaction**

In the front stage, one of the few alternatives available to improve productivity is reducing the length or the intensity of interaction.

This is a questionable option for high-contact services. Should a hairdresser cut hair faster to reduce the "cycle time" and improve the turnover? "No, no, my head is unique. Take your time!" would be the customer's answer. To reduce the intensity of interaction, lower-paid assistants could help the professional, washing the hair and doing menial tasks. Another solution is to convince the customer to do part of the job – maybe wash his hair himself. This is "co-production," a term that is often preferred to "self-service."

So a good way to reduce the intensity of interaction is to play on the process dimension (cycle time, simplification of the interaction) and on the people dimension (expertise leverage, co-production).

There is a huge cost difference between a face-to-face interaction with an expert, a telephone call and a web transaction. New technology may be used to automate the process, as with automatic teller machines at banks or optical scanning systems in supermarkets. In many cases, this is possible only with the help and expertise of the customer himself, who does part of the job.

THE SERVICE-INTENSITY MATRIX

The service-intensity matrix is obtained by combining these two dimensions (outcome and intensity). This matrix is very useful for positioning services in the same industry, which would be expected to fall along the diagonal of the matrix given the correlation between customization and high interaction in the upper left corner of the matrix and standardization and low interaction in the bottom right corner.

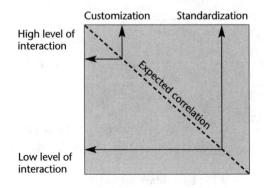

FIGURE 4.4 **The service-intensity matrix**

43

This can be observed in the hotel business, for example. The various hotel brands of the Accor Group fall nicely along the diagonal, as the average price of the room moves down by regular amounts.

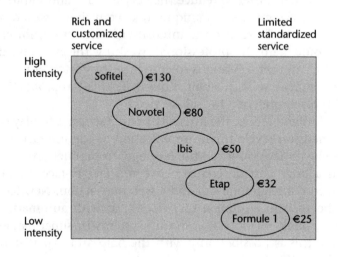

FIGURE 4.5 **Accor hotels**

The intensity of interaction can also be measured in the number of employees per room, as shown for Marriott hotels.

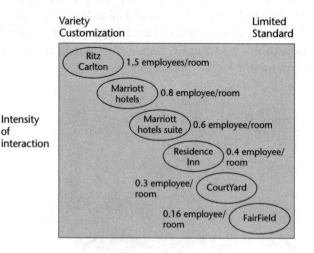

FIGURE 4.6 **Marriott hotels**

The main advantage of the service-intensity matrix is to display three essential and interdependent dimensions of the service mix: product, process and people. As communications theorist and writer Marshall McLuhan[1] used to say, the medium is the message – we could say the process is the product and the product is the process. It is important to show the interplay of these elements on the same picture.

THE PRODUCT/PROCESS MATRIX IN THE BACK STAGE

The quest for productivity in the back stage is clearly demonstrated on the product/process matrix described by Bob Hayes and Steve Wheelwright;[2] Figure 4.7 is a simplified version. The horizontal axis represents the normal evolution from the initial appearance of a product in its customized form to the mature stage, where it becomes a commodity. The vertical axis represents the main production processes: project, workshop and batch production, line production and continuous flow.

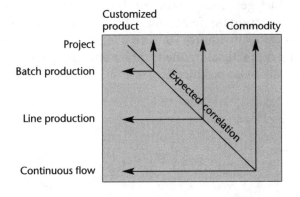

FIGURE 4.7 **Product/process matrix**

Once again, products move down along the diagonal as they become commodities and are mass-produced.

Customized products and small series are manufactured in workshops where similar operations are grouped together by functions. This functional organization is found in print shops, garages and kitchens of traditional restaurants (Figure 4.8).

45

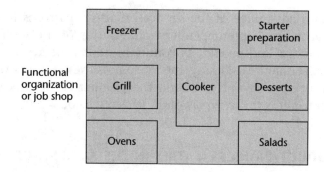

FIGURE 4.8 **Kitchen of a traditional restaurant**

The main advantage of a functional organization is flexibility. A wide variety of dishes can be prepared à la carte, at the demand of customers. But the required flexibility in the back stage rapidly becomes a nightmare in terms of scheduling and shifting bottlenecks. Costs are high, as capacity utilization is low and skilled operators expensive.

As the product gets more standard, less flexibility is needed. The sequence of operations is fixed along the production line. Capacity utilization is drastically improved, with a regular flow of products, and the scheduling is greatly simplified. Larger and larger volumes of standard products are mass-produced.

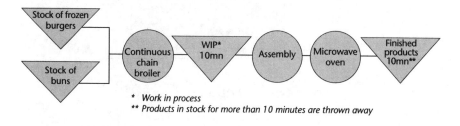

* Work in process
** Products in stock for more than 10 minutes are thrown away

FIGURE 4.9 **Fast-food production line**

The last position on the diagonal (Figure 4.7) is continuous flow, which is the dream of industrial engineers. Great investments in huge production units bring large economies of scale. Standard products such as steel, flat glass and paper continuously flow along rigid processes. But as the product becomes more and more standard, the only possibility of differentiation becomes price, and a vicious circle is set in motion: price reduction leads to cost reduction and economies of scale. Economies of scale are obtained with greater capacity. Greater capacity means more things to sell, which in turn leads to lower prices, further cost cutting and even greater capacity.

One of the few possibilities for escaping this vicious cycle is customizing the product and selling solutions with more service. Back-stage operations and production lines have to become more flexible. Now every car is different at the end of the line.

Mass customization is usually obtained by modular design or post-poned differentiation. Personal computers are assembled from a combination of standard modules: disks, printed circuit boards, specific software. The same platform is used for different models of cars in the same family and is kept standard as long as possible; differentiation into final products occurs as late as possible.

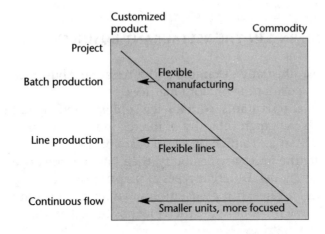

FIGURE 4.10 **Flexibility in the back stage**

This analysis could be extended to any back-stage operations. Retail banks have automated their back offices, enabling them to service a virtually unlimited number of transactions at a negligible marginal cost. With the flexibility brought by information technology, they are able to deliver customized applications for automated lending, credit card operations or similar transactions. But this massive processing of information, on the production-line mode, remains rather rigid. Corporate or private banking may have to resort to more flexible processes, on the workshop or functional mode.

When operations are quite standardized, they may be outsourced locally (onshore) if they still need to remain rather close to the front stage because of the complexity of the interaction or the need of local knowledge.

If the back-stage activities are not constrained by local or front-stage requirements, they can be offshored anywhere in the world. For example, an airline may decide to relocate its accounts-receivable and collections functions to India.

Relocating back-office jobs is not new but the lowering of bandwidth and telecommunication costs have made it possible to offshore activities farther afield, to lower-wage locations.

The service-intensity matrix and the product/process matrix are useful instruments that can be used in any kind of industry, as will be shown in the following examples.

POSITIONING IN THE RESTAURANT BUSINESS

The most illustrative example is the restaurant business; Figure 4.11 shows its positioning on both matrices.

Gourmet restaurants, which sell a sophisticated menu in a pleasant setting, have a high intensity of interaction with a number of professional waiters and a high degree of customization with a varied menu. To ensure the necessary flexibility, their kitchens are organized on the workshop model. Different types of preparation are grouped together: pastry in one area, fish preparation in another, sauces in a corner and so on. These restaurants are therefore positioned on the top left corner of the two matrices.

In fast-food restaurants, the low intensity of interaction is in line with the high degree of standardization of the food offered. In the kitchen, the food is prepared along traditional production lines. Fast-food outlets are therefore positioned in the bottom right corner of the two matrices.

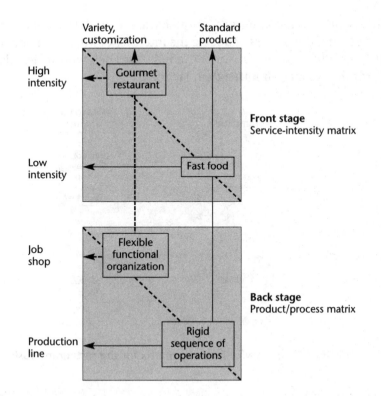

FIGURE 4.11 **Front-stage and back-stage matrices for the restaurant business**

Exploring the service-intensity matrix

When Rocky Aoki, the Japanese founder of Benihana, arrived in America, he had a dream: introduce Japanese-style grills to Americans. The customer was to enjoy a memorable and reassuring experience of Japanese cuisine while being entertained by the chef in the front stage.

Where is the Benihana restaurant positioned on the matrix?

It is clearly in the top right corner, as the product is rather standard (a simple combination of grilled items) but the level of interaction is quite high; the chef interacts directly with the customer while putting on a show.

But is this position sustainable?

As the interaction with the chef and the show become less original and the concept becomes less innovative and more copied by the competition, Benihana's position will shift further to the right. Are customers still willing to pay the same price for a service that has lost its newness?

The position is less and less comfortable and contenders will compete by simplifying the process, reducing the intensity of interaction and cutting the price. To do so they may, for example, use chefs who are less skilled or hire other Asian staff rather than Japanese.

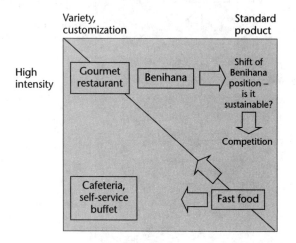

FIGURE 4.12 **The service-intensity matrix for the restaurant business**

On the other hand, being in the bottom right corner is not more comfortable. As the service offering gets very standard, the main competitive differentiator is price. What are the options? One option is to become number one or two in the industry to benefit from economies of scale in the back stage. Another option is to increase the scope and the variety of the offering by introducing a more differentiated menu or other services, such as playgrounds for children. A third option is to ask the customer do part of the job (that is, prepare his or her own plate according to needs or desires) and move to the bottom left corner, where self-service buffet and cafeteria services are to be found. But are customers willing to do the job to get more customization? Some will, and this is a good base for segmentation.

POSITIONING IN E-BUSINESS

It is worthwhile exploring further the process/people dimension of the service-intensity matrix. The most intense and expensive interaction is a face-to-face with an expert; the least intense and expensive is a simple online link between two computers on the web. The cost difference is huge and is not always justified, as a face-to-face with an expert is not necessarily better than a face-to-face with a teller equipped with an expert system, and an interaction with a teller is not necessarily better than an interaction with an automatic teller machine. A phone call is not necessarily better than an e-mail.

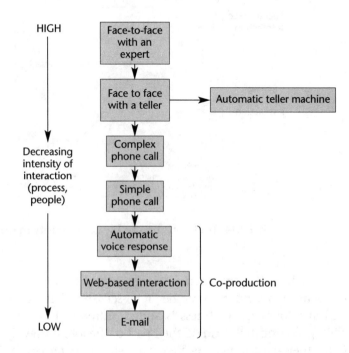

FIGURE 4.13 **Decreasing intensity of interaction**

To get cash the customer may prefer to use an ATM rather than go inside the branch and wait in line. The machine is polite and predictable and speaks any language.

It is worth noting that as the interaction with the employee is reduced, the participation and the involvement of the customer are increased.

With this detailed process/people dimension in place, the service-intensity matrix can explain the outburst of e-services brought by the net economy and the information technology revolution.

Traditionally, business services moved along the diagonal of the matrix, trading richness of relationship with a few customers in the top left corner for standardized transactions with many customers in the bottom right. Richness has to be sacrificed to increase reach.

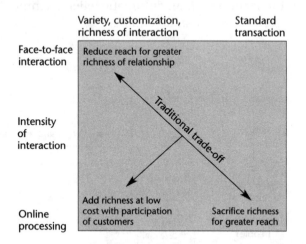

FIGURE 4.14 **Trade-offs on the service-intensity matrix**

But when the interaction deals with bits (and not atoms and molecules), information can be processed, stored, enriched and customized at a low cost. Richness is added online as long as customers are willing to contribute and do their part of the job. If they do not have the skills, they have to be educated. The e-business moves to the lower left corner of the matrix.

POSITIONING IN FINANCIAL SERVICES

When a number of internet brokerage sites suddenly appeared in cyberspace and enabled clients to buy and sell stocks for a fraction of what a traditional broker used to charge and also gave them quotes, financial and market analysis, and online portfolio tracking for free, Merrill Lynch realized that to survive it had to get smarter as a broker and offer real value-added service to its clients. It had to better segment its clients and provide more high-touch personal advice and full service.

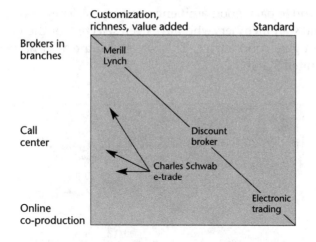

FIGURE 4.15 **Financial services on the service-intensity matrix**

American discount broker Charles Schwab provides personalized and customized relationships online and by phone, but it has found that its customers like to open their accounts in branches, even if they later deal online. Charles Schwab thus provides the three communication channels: face-to-face, call center and online. It is the customer who does the job and decides which channel to use.

In an e-business environment, the winners offer customers all the channels – "clicks and mortar." The branch is not dead; it is just another channel. But all channels have to be fully integrated to provide a seamless interaction.

POSITIONING IN BOOK RETAILING

Traditional bookstores that simply sell a limited range of books do not have a bright future. Location close to the customer is still an advantage, but in the matrix they appear in the top middle, shifting to the right. Their customers are less and less ready to pay the price of a face-to-face interaction for a transaction that could be done more cheaply in a supermarket.

A better solution is a move to the left, either to superstores or to e-business. Superstores offer a rich purchase experience by stocking more than 150,000 books, furnishing armchairs and reading tables, and providing coffee bars, good ambience and music. They stay open late at night, and staff members who have been selected for their interest in books can give good advice. This was the strategy of Barnes & Noble in the United States.

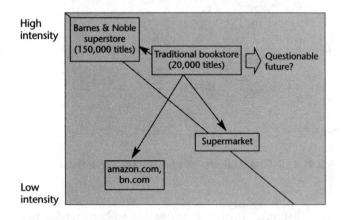

FIGURE 4.16 **Book retailing on the service-intensity matrix**

At the other end, Amazon.com gives access to millions of books while offering advice based on the interest profile of the customer or impartial information provided by other customers who have read the book. The competition forced Barnes & Noble to create the site bn.com to give customers the choice between clicks and mortar.

It is important to note that a click of the mouse in the front stage prompts a physical movement of books in the back stage. Front-stage transactions have to be supported by high-performing back-stage operations with warehouses, logistics, partnerships and so on.

POSITIONING IN CONSULTING BUSINESS

In the consulting business, the intensity of interaction is best expressed by the level of expertise of professionals. The classification of David Maister[3] describes three types of project work: Brain, Gray Hair, and Procedure.

Brain projects require expert professionals. The client's project involves major, complex, innovative issues, requiring state-of-the-art, professional knowledge.

Gray Hair projects require experienced professionals who are able to customize and adapt solutions that are not completely new and have been developed in other industries.

Procedure projects address well-recognized and familiar issues.

It is important to position the client's demand on this matrix, because all aspects of the service proposition are affected, particularly the composition of the team (the right mix of expert, experienced and junior professionals) and, most important, the price. This is a dynamic positioning, as over time, Brain projects become Gray Hair projects and, eventually, Procedure projects. Manual accounting processes that were ill-specified and considered complex in the 1950s have become routine with the integration of computerized accounting and payroll systems. The same evolution can be seen in systems integration and now in business integration. Moving up the value chain and doing higher value-added business is a central concern of most consulting businesses to maintain differentiation and higher fees.

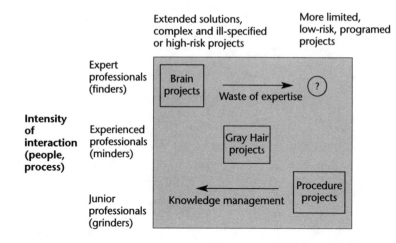

FIGURE 4.17 **Consulting business on the service-intensity matrix**

Consultants have to be careful not to waste precious professional expertise on projects that are becoming more standard and routine. On the other hand, efficiency can be increased by more rapidly developing the professionalism of junior staff with expert systems and knowledge management.

CONCLUSION

Although rather simple and unsophisticated, the service-intensity matrix is a robust instrument that can be used for any type of service. It allows an initial positioning according to three dimensions: product, process and people. The people dimension concerns front-liners and customers who exchange their roles as shown on the service triangle. As customers are led to co-produce and participate, they have to be trained and rewarded. It is possible to take this positioning further with customer segmentation and a more extensive service proposition. This is the subject of the next chapter.

FINDING AND KEEPING THE FIT

The service-intensity matrix is a good instrument to use for a first positioning of the service concept. The next step is to design a proposition that will fit the needs of the main stakeholders: the customer, the employee and the firm.

How specific should the proposition be to offer the proper value to each individual customer and employee? But how large and homogeneous should the target segment be to bring good value to the firm?

SEGMENTATION AND FOCUS

As the front stage grows in importance, the traditional "product" segmentation has to be extended to take into account the service experience. The more customers are involved in the interaction, the more it becomes necessary to consider the occasion of the encounter, the role they will play, their mode of participation and their level of expertise. For example, customers traveling for business and those traveling for leisure are treated differently. Restaurants in an airport should deal differently with customers who are in a hurry and those who have time to spare. Some clients may want full service from their brokers; others have the time or the expertise to do the job themselves on the web.

Once the segmentation is established, every aspect of the service proposition should be designed to fit the needs of customers in the chosen segment. For example, if the airport restaurant targets people who are in a hurry, the six P's of the service mix should be designed to respond to this objective (simple menu, easy access, speed, and so on). But the other two stakeholders should not be forgotten. The firm should make a profit, and the employees should be content with their working environment.

Shouldice Hospital, a long-established private hospital in Toronto, treats only one type of patient: those suffering from inguinal hernia. It has specialized to the extent that it turns down hernia patients who are overweight or have a history of heart trouble. With such a narrow segment, the operations are well focused. The treatment is fairly standardized, and surgeons have become highly proficient and effective through repetition and focused continuous improvement. Patients are given a local anesthetic and can walk to a wheelchair right after surgery. The environment is pleasant, and the hospital looks more like a country club, with no smell of disinfectant. The risers on the stairs are low, to help patients walk around more easily. All the P's of the service mix have been designed concurrently to focus on this segment and to maximize value.

The *value to patients* is that their hernias are repaired effectively. Moreover, the experience is memorable and recovery fast. The *value to the hospital* is the cost reduction brought about by the standardization of operations and equipment, the participation of patients and the good utilization of capacity and resources. The *value to the staff* is pleasant working conditions, less stress and good results. Value is well balanced among the three stakeholders.

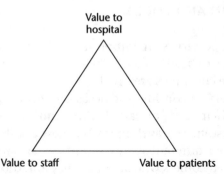

FIGURE 5.1 **Value to the three stakeholders of the service triangle**

VALUE TO CUSTOMER

The first task is to consider the fit between the key operating decisions of the service mix and what customers value. Value is the result of the comparison between perceived benefits and perceived sacrifices, one obvious sacrifice being the willingness to pay the price.

First of all, the customer is concerned with the outcome. He wants to get the expected results with the right level of professionalism. But he is also sensitive to the tangible elements that convey assurance and make the encounter memorable and special. He may appreciate the empathy of the staff and the permanence of the relationship. He will prize the responsiveness and availability of people as well as the speed and ease of the interaction. Finally, he will expect consistency of operations across locations and time. All these benefits will add up and determine his willingness to pay for the service.

A simple example will show how the six elements of the service mix should be designed to maximize benefits and minimize sacrifices. The idea of Rocky Aoki, the Japanese founder of Benihana, was to introduce Japanese-style grills to Americans. The customer would enjoy a memorable experience while being served and entertained by the chef, all at a reasonable price. It is remarkable to see how Aoki designed some of the key elements of the service proposition to offer very high value to the customer. He certainly used more intuition than formal analysis, but the result was an outstanding breakthrough. The most significant decisions were:

- *Product:* there was a short, simple menu with few variations.
- *Location:* restaurants were sited in busy traffic zones to ensure a good utilization of capacity.
- *Process:* the chef was brought from the back stage to the dining room to cook in front of a table of eight guests and put on a well-prepared show that contributed to the memorable experience. A large bar functioned as a buffer that absorbed variations in demand and held customers waiting for a table.
- *People:* the chef played several roles – taking orders, cooking, serving and entertaining the guests. He controlled the speed of "delivery" and the quality of the interaction. He was in charge of the whole experience.

The fit between value to customer and service proposition appears clearly on a matrix where the two dimensions, value to customer and service mix, have been displayed vertically and horizontally (see Figure 5.2).

Regrouping all elements on the same matrix reveals the coherence of Benihana's proposition. It is this fit that distinguishes breakthrough services.

Any service can be analyzed with a more generic matrix, depicted in Figure 5.3.

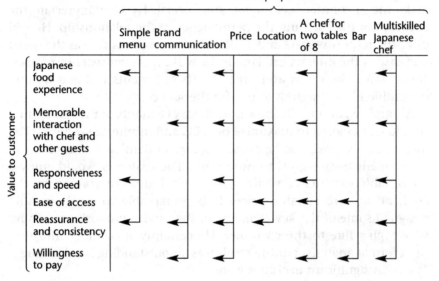

FIGURE 5.2 **Finding the fit for Benihana restaurants**

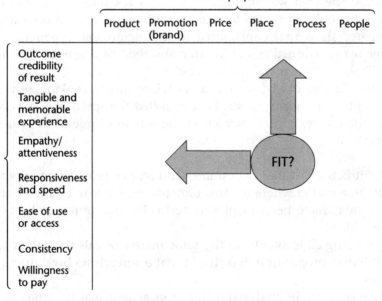

FIGURE 5.3 **Maximizing value to customers**

VALUE TO EMPLOYEES

Since employees are involved in producing, delivering and marketing the service, it is important to evaluate the impact of the service proposition on them. Operating decisions may affect their job concerns, such as career and compensation, working conditions, participation and initiative. They may also affect more personal motivations, such as sense of belonging, self-esteem, aspiration for growth and challenge.

Again the good fit for Benihana can be displayed on the matrix shown in Figure 5.4.

The fact that all chefs are Japanese increases their sense of belonging. The multiplicity of roles and the challenge to deliver a good show play on their job concerns as well as their motivation.

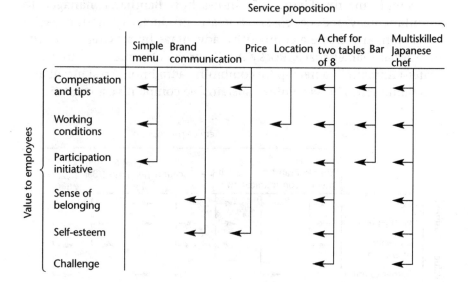

FIGURE 5.4 **Maximizing value to employees**

VALUE TO BUSINESS

A business firm is not a philanthropic organization, so the service proposition should bring value to the business as well. There are three main dimensions: cost/productivity, capacity utilization and barrier to entry. How does the service proposition help the organization build a strong and sustainable competitive position?

In the case of Benihana, low cost results from the simplicity of the menu, which allows reduced stocks and less waste.

Productivity derives from the reduced "cycle time" (the average length of a meal is 45 minutes), the fact that the chef serves two tables of eight (and so sixteen diners) at a time, and the chef's ability to perform a number of tasks and play different roles.

What are the elements of the value proposition that could bring a sustainable competitive advantage? The choice of good locations offers the possibility of preempting the best sites. The staff are the resource that is most difficult to replicate, as the selection, training and motivation of the chefs take time to develop. Finally, the fit itself, the integration and combination of all decisions, may constitute the most important advantage.

A simple matrix (Figure 5.5) shows how Benihana managed to simultaneously reduce costs, increase productivity and capacity utilization, and create a competitive advantage by moving out of the traditional market space. Rocky Aoki's stroke of genius was to create "eater-tainment" – a new space combining a traditional restaurant and entertainment. This gave him a sustainable competitive advantage.

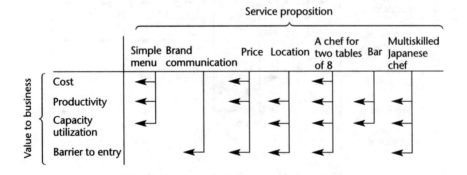

FIGURE 5.5 **Maximizing value to business**

THE FIT

A breakthrough service – a winning proposition – has to achieve a strong fit and a good balance of value perceived by the three stakeholders: the firm, the staff and the customer. This is clearly visible on the service triangle (Figure 5.6).

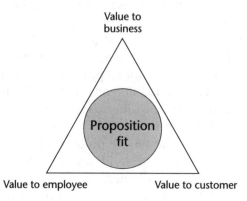

FIGURE 5.6 **Value to the three stakeholders of the service triangle**

FROM SERVICE PROPOSITION TO SERVICE DELIVERY

The next imperative is to develop resources and product capabilities inside the organization to deliver the promised proposition at a good price. To maximize margin, costs have to be pushed down and capacity utilization optimized. This comes from the design of proper products and solutions, the balance between front and back activities at different moments and in different locations, and the balance between demand and capacity (this will be developed in Chapter 7). Resources are mainly people, so the selection and training of staff and customers is of paramount importance. Their motivation and loyalty will be highly dependent on systems and procedures, management style and shared values.

For example, in the case of the Benihana chain, the most important resource is the frontline staff. Chefs have to be carefully selected and trained. Other aspects – systems, job design, management style – support the central role of the chef.

COMMODITIZATION AND SURVIVAL OF THE FITTEST

Alas – nothing fails like success! A good fit will not last forever.

Competitors will readily copy the successful formula, customers will get used to it, the proposition will soon become commonplace, and it will be essential to redesign it, to re-create value and move away from commoditization and price war.

But there is a paradox here: the stronger the fit, the more difficult it will be to unravel it and deviate from it. One solution is to stay within the same market space and look for a "plus," a competitive advantage that could make a significant difference. But if the market space is crowded, this element may be readily copied. In the restaurant business, the traditional solution is to regularly redesign the menu, renovate the house or simplify the service proposition. Benihana added a new chain of grill restaurants; they fit smaller spaces and cost one-third of a traditional Benihana to build.

Another solution is to create a new service proposition by expanding the boundaries of the existing market space, moving beyond traditional competition by inventing new rules of the game. This is what Benihana tried with a "new" concept bridging bar and restaurant (the concept was actually imported from Japan). At Sushi Doraku (which derives its name from the Japanese words for "joy of sushi"), patrons seated at a large oval marble bar serve themselves from an ingenious conveyor-belt system revolving inside the bar. Scores of combinations of fresh fish, seafood, rice and vegetables pass as diners make their selections. Prices are indicated by the color-coded serving plates, and the bill is calculated by adding up the price of the empty colored plates at the guest's place. With Sushi Doraku bars, Benihana was able to further expand the boundaries of the "eater-tainment" market space it had pioneered more than 30 years before.

THE VALUE CREATION CYCLE

The devil is in the detail. As a single detail can make a significant difference, it is essential to watch over the customer to understand how value is created at each moment of truth over what Sandra Vandermerwe[1] calls the "customer activity cycle" – what I prefer to call the "value creation cycle." For example, the value creation cycle in the hotel business is depicted in Figure 5.7 and lists the possible customer needs.

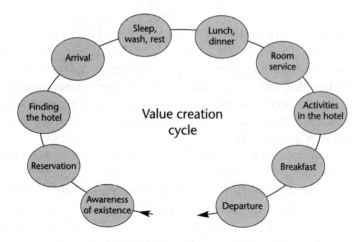

FIGURE 5.7 **Value creation cycle in the hotel business**

The service proposition has to be further detailed. How many activities should be covered, with what level of customization and staff interaction?

Full-service hotels in the luxury segment will cover the full range of activities of the cycle, whereas hotels in the economy segment may cover only the basic amenities, reducing frontline contact to a minimum and resorting to co-production as often as possible (Figure 5.8).

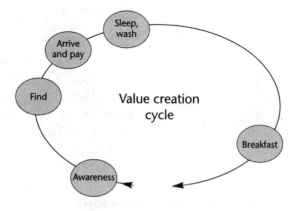

FIGURE 5.8 **Value creation cycle for budget hotels**

The service proposition is constructed step by step by under-standing what targeted customers value at each encounter and deciding what to offer. For example, at arrival the choice is very wide – from guests who expect to be welcomed day and night by a receptionist who will recognize them and remember their prefer-ences to "functional" travelers who are content with an interaction with a machine that takes information and a credit card and then delivers a plastic room key.

At each key moment of truth, there are many ways to make a differ-ence, as can be seen in Figure 5.9 for a full-service hotel: how much front-stage interaction, how much customization, what level of co-production, which activities should be shifted to the back stage?

The choice is vast but fortunately restricted by cultural habits and expectations. Each decision has implications for capabilities, resources and systems, and finally the price of the proposition after integration of all elements. As mentioned above, a good balance has to be found between value to customer, value to employee and value to business.

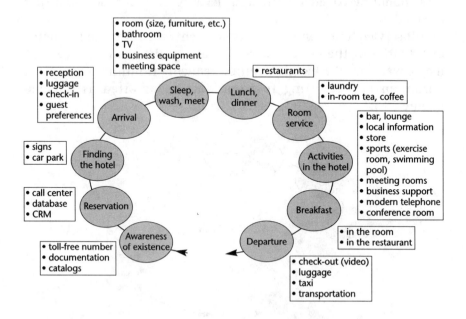

FIGURE 5.9 **Full-service hotel**

CREATING ELEMENTS OF DIFFERENTIATION IN THE VALUE CREATION CYCLE

The value creation cycle is a good instrument to help find out at each key moment of interaction how to create and build customer value while reducing cost. This is simply value analysis (a good old method traditionally used by engineers for product design) conducted systematically along the cycle. Each element of the proposition is analyzed to determine whether it can be eliminated or reduced because it is not valued by the customer or whether it should be enhanced or another element added to create a determinant difference.

Formule 1, in the low-budget hotel industry, was able to differentiate itself from competitors in the same sector by focusing on a few key interactions and delivering superior value at these moments of truth. They were able to create differences that stuck out and were highly valued.

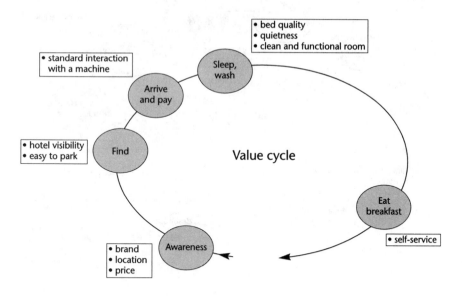

FIGURE 5.10 **Formule 1 hotels**

These moments of truth were supported by strong elements of the service mix:

- Strong brand
- Good locations
- Hotel built from basic prefabricated modules of four standard rooms
- The ability to add capacity by simply adding modules
- Back-stage organization and support systems (economies of scale)
- Local management by a married couple responsible for hiring and managing a few employees and part-timers

The same value cycle illustrates how Richard Branson tried to create critical and visible elements of differentiation for Virgin Atlantic Airlines.

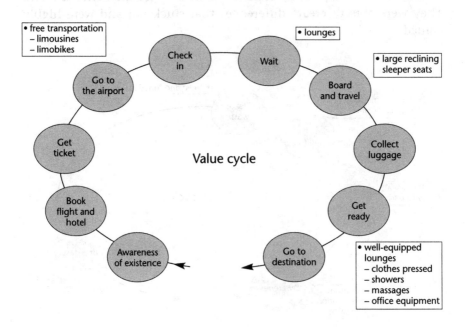

FIGURE 5.11 **Elements of differentiation for Virgin Atlantic**

Are they creating a sustainable difference? Are customers willing to pay over time? Sooner or later successful ideas are copied and new ways are to be found to re-create value or reduce cost.

CONCLUSION

In summary, the operative strategy consists of defining the key elements of the service mix to maximize value to customer, value to employee and value to firm. It is important to focus on key sustainable competitive advantages by extending this analysis to the main moments of interaction in the value creation cycle. The next step is to infer from this analysis the necessary resources, capabilities and systems.

QUALITY GAPS

Quality of service is different from quality of product. No matter how much care is taken in designing the service on paper, in testing it and in delivering it, what customers perceive is quite different from the original proposition. Again, the service triangle will be a good instrument to bring the resulting quality gaps to the fore.

THE DESIGN GAP

The service concept, born from analysis of needs, segmentation and marketing studies, is transformed into a proposition formulated according to the service mix (product/outcome, price, place/location, process/layout and capacity, and people/style and behavior).

This is represented as a square at the top of the service triangle, as it has been designed by "squared" people who have to specify it with standards and quantitative measurements. Obviously, there will always remain a gap between this squared offering and the fluid, varied and changing demand of an individual customer represented by a circle.

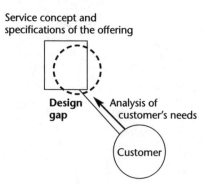

FIGURE 6.1 **Design gap**

THE DELIVERY GAP

Employees have to deliver the service at specific moments of truth within the perimeter of the square and according to the rulebook of their profession. They will do it with more or less success. There will be minuses if the delivery is not up to the specifications or the rules, and pluses if the employee goes that extra mile to please the customer, or if the professional works minor miracles to adjust to the situation.

Big mistakes and little miracles are variations around the proposed perimeter. Employees may color outside the lines, but they still have to remain within the square.

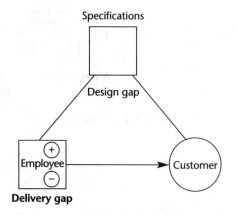

FIGURE 6.2 **Delivery gap**

If they remain inside the specified box, employees may lose sight of customers' needs. The technical orientation of service providers may favor internal objectives that will facilitate their jobs but at the expense of customer satisfaction. For example, filling out long and complicated forms helps the organization but punishes the customer.

THE PERCEPTION GAP

The next gap comes from the fact that the customer perceives only a part of the square, a part of the offering. He may not be able to fully perceive the technical aspect of the service.

For example, a doctor may be extremely concerned by the technical aspect of the treatment. The patient may be more responsive to the care aspect of the process than to the cure aspect: quality of life after the treatment, speed of recovery or explanations in understandable terms.

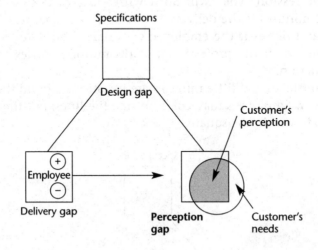

FIGURE 6.3 **Perception gap**

Quality is what customers say it is, and their perception is their reality. What they do not perceive has little value in their eyes, and they are not willing to pay for it. Value is the ratio between perceived benefits and perceived sacrifices (for example money, time and effort).

THE FILTERS OF PERCEPTION

Perception is not a rational process. It is shaped by a series of filters or biases (Figure 6.4).

Frame of reference

We look at the world with our own specific lenses through which impressions are formed. We develop our own grammar to interpret the world through our language, our culture, our experience, our lifestyle. We are, for example, optimistic or pessimistic. And those patterns are reinforced by habit. Available frames of reference are consonant with what is familiar, memorable and above all has emotional significance.

Confirmation bias

We see what we believe. We tend to see confirmation of our opinions and cling to them, especially when they are reinforced by the group. We gather information that supports our beliefs and discount, deny or ignore what disturbs them. Those beliefs often originate from first impressions or are anchored by recent imprints, available or vivid memories.

For example, initial contacts are of particular importance. Restaurant managers know that when a customer sits down unhappy, he will make trouble and complain all evening. In some organizations, the receptionist is called the "director of first impressions." And once a customer has formed an opinion, it remains firmly rooted in his mind and is difficult to change.

Overgeneralization and categorization

We tend to integrate, condense and categorize our perceptions to form simpler representations and global judgments. It is all or nothing; it is black or white; we like it or we don't.

A service is made up of many moments of truth, but with the integrative capacity of our mind, we form a single overall impression. We fill the gaps and construct a global opinion. It is much like a bank account: when the job is right, the customer credits the account, and in case of mistake he debits it – but one debit counts for more than ten credits. So the more contacts, the greater the chances of failure!

As most details are dropped and the remaining few are sharpened, we jump easily to a definitive conclusion from a single impression. The first impression, the last impression or the memory of an emotional moment may color the whole experience. We blow things out of proportion and exaggerate small details. A single negative element could ruin the whole experience. Because the checkout assistant was unpleasant this time, we may decide never to return to that particular store.

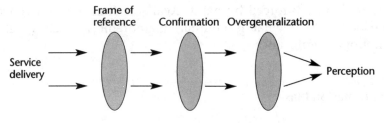

FIGURE 6.4 **Filters of perception**

EXPECTATIONS

Once the service offering has been defined, it is communicated to customers, in whom it induces expectations. Obviously, the firm has to choose the aspects of the service it wants to communicate from among many possible dimensions, and the promises it makes should relate to tangible and differentiating aspects. This is done through traditional media channels such as advertising, mailing or brochures, and is reinforced by a strong brand and image.

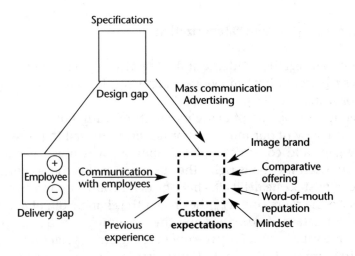

FIGURE 6.5 **Customer expectations**

But the firm communicates best during the service interaction. Everything it does or says about itself through the delivery process and the frontline staff is a form of communication. Moreover, word of mouth, which reflects actual customer experience, may have a greater impact on expectations than traditional media. Finally, if the customer has already tried the service or tested a similar one, this experience will play a major role in shaping his expectations.

THE VALUE GAP

Finally, the satisfaction of the customer and his willingness to pay for the service result from the comparison between perception and expectation. This comparison is a complex operation, but it can be represented simply.

Value gap = perception–expectation

This is a subjective construct, biased by perception filters – fluid, inconsistent and whimsical. But as we shall see later, it is essential to encourage employees to be aware of the value gap. This will help them be more proactive, enhance perception and readjust expectations, underpromise and overdeliver.

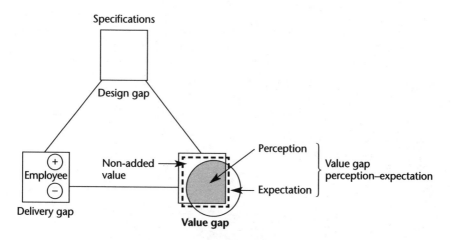

FIGURE 6.6 **Value gap**

CONCLUSION

Quality of product in the back stage is about conformity, but in the front stage, quality of service strives to reduce the three gaps: design, delivery and value. Those three gaps are easy to relate to the corners of the service triangle, which is an invaluable representation to explain the special nature of services.

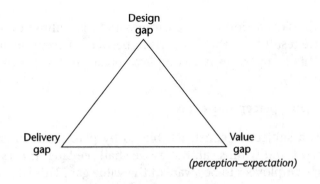

FIGURE 6.7 **The three quality gaps**

7

THE THREE MOVEMENTS OF QUALITY

At the core of any approach to quality, there are three basic mechanisms, three movements that interlock to bring value to the customer. These three movements are taken apart and analyzed separately in this chapter, but they need to be considered under the same umbrella and connected by a dynamic change process, be it TQM, Kaizen, Six Sigma or Change Acceleration Process.

The first movement is about doing the *thing right* in the back stage as well as in the front stage. The second movement is about doing the *right thing* for the customer – that is, filling the value gap between perception and expectations. And this sets in motion the third movement, the improvement and differentiation that enable the voice of the customer to be heard inside the organization, upstream along business processes to the far corners of the back stage.

THE FIRST MOVEMENT: EVERYONE IS RESPONSIBLE FOR DOING THE THING RIGHT

Back-stage operations

The story starts in the back stage with a tangible product. The product is represented with a square because it has been designed by "squared" people, people with a squared vision, obsessed with standards, specifications, tolerances and quantitative measurements.

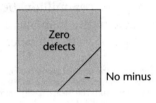

FIGURE 7.1 **Zero defects**

Doing the thing right implies zero defects or error-free work, but this does not mean perfection; it implies that the main characteristics of the product should stay within acceptable tolerance limits. The manufacturing of a product is a random phenomenon. When the production process is under control, the final dimensions are the result of small and random common causes of variation that add together to give a "normal" distribution, the well-known bell-shaped curve. Results are symmetrically distributed around the nominal value, and dispersion is measured by the standard deviation "sigma" (the Greek letter σ).

As long as the product dimensions remain within the designed tolerance limits, the product is good, and all products whose characteristics are within the tolerance limits are equally good. Outside these limits, products are considered defective and must be scrapped or repaired at a cost.[i]

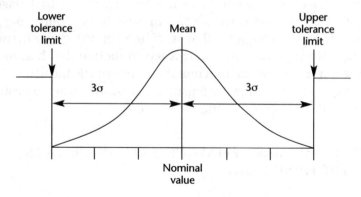

FIGURE 7.2 **Limits at 3σ**

When the tolerances are set at three standard deviations from the mean, 0.135 defective products per hundred are expected on each side of the distribution. A percentage of 0.135 may look reasonable, but 0.135 percent converted into parts per million becomes 1,350 parts per million. This is unacceptable in the manufacturing of complex systems made up of thousands of parts! With tolerances at four standard devia-

---

i Actually, the closer the characteristics of the product are to the nominal value, the better. According to Genichi Taguchi, quality consists of minimizing the loss inflicted by the product not only on the customer, but also on society in the long run. The main source of that loss is variability, the absolute evil. Zero dispersion at nominal value is morally right!

tions, the defect rate falls to 30 defects per million (30 chances in a million to get a part outside limits). But with six standard deviations, the defect rate is essentially zero, zero parts per million.[ii] A dream! And Six Sigma, the buzzword at Motorola and then at GE, spreads rapidly.

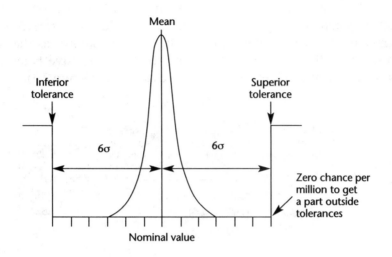

FIGURE 7.3 **Limits at 6σ**

Variability is the enemy that must be crushed to do the thing right. But how is it possible to achieve this extraordinary level of quality? Is it possible to inspect or sample to find a single defective part in a box containing one million items? Clearly not. There is only one possible approach to this challenge: the famous SPC, Statistical Process Control, brought to Japan in 1950 by Edward Deming.[1] His message was simple: "Move from mass inspection to process control."

The best way to explain the SPC approach is to take a very simple example: you are to produce one million traditional English puddings a day with zero defects. All key final characteristics of the puddings are to be within specified tolerances.

Where quantification is possible, each specification is expressed in terms of a nominal value and a tolerance range showing acceptable variation. (For some characteristics, quantification is so difficult that operators are forced to make do with qualitative judgment, but this is

ii In each case of a shift of the mean of 1.5σ (wearing of the tool, for example), the defect rate can reach 3.4 parts per million.

another problem.) For example, the height of the pudding should have a nominal value of 10 centimeters and tolerances between 9.9 and 10.1 centimeters.

The solution is to identify the key process parameters that affect the results. At the beginning, a large number of parameters appear to influence the final characteristics of the product, but on closer scrutiny and after systematic experimentation, few determining variables will emerge. The well-known fishbone diagram, also known as the cause-and-effect diagram, can help isolate these few decisive parameters, which are generally regrouped into five categories (Figure 7.4).

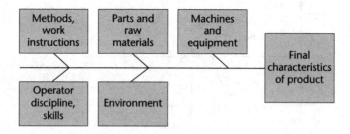

FIGURE 7.4 **Fishbone diagram for a back-stage process**

Fishbone, or cause-and-effect, diagram[2]

The first idea that comes to mind is to control the quality of key ingredients and carefully define the acceptable variation limits of the raw materials. This requires systematic experimentation and correlation analysis linking process parameters to final characteristics. The next step is to define the proportions of those ingredients and the recipe. Then come machines and equipment: acceptable limits of variation for the temperature in the oven or cooking time. As long as the decisive parameters are maintained within precise variation limits and the operators comply with specific procedures, the final characteristics of the product will be right the first time and every time.

Control of final results by inspection (which is too late and very expensive) has been replaced by direct process control. This needs an upstream investment in prevention, know-how and learning, which will be recovered through future savings in inspection, failure, correction and guarantee costs, not to mention customer goodwill. When a final characteristic goes beyond the predetermined limits, products have to be inspected and sorted. This is the price to be paid for ignorance about the process. However, though trial and error may seem a crude and inefficient method, it is the only possible solution when the process is not fully understood.

To keep the process under control, operators must regularly measure the final results; as soon as one characteristic exceeds the predetermined control limits, they must stop and correct the process to understand the causes of variation. They must find out which parameter to adjust to set things right. In this way they learn more about the process and accumulate knowledge in the form of standards and checklists. This is how they hold on to the learning, the gain.

But who decided that the tolerances for the height of the pudding should be 10 ± 0.1 centimeters? Marketing and design teams. For a number of reasons, they may now decide to reduce variation to ± 0.05 centimeters. This will make things difficult for the operators, as they will have to do more experiments to find out which parameters to adjust to comply with the new demand.

As can be seen by this simple example, neither standards nor operating procedures are permanent. They must be regularly adjusted, updated and validated by all parties. The solution is prevention and learning at every stage of development or production. Everyone is responsible for quality, for controlling his own process.

The problem with the SPC approach is that it looks quite technical and often turns off managers who prefer to speak the language of money and business results. So consultants have widely used the cost-of-quality concept to demonstrate that quality is an economic solution and means good business.

This is not a cost-cutting approach – the so-called "cheese slicer" approach, which consists of cutting more or less the same amount of costs uniformly across the organization. The idea is to invest up front in prevention to reduce appraisal and failure costs at later stages. The cost of quality is made up of four costs:

- *Prevention costs:* project reviews, design reviews, validation, training maintenance, improvement projects, designs of experiments, operating procedures, guidelines, and so on – it's about learning, anticipation, knowledge.
- *Appraisal costs:* tests, inspection, audit surveys, processing control data, reports, evaluation of suppliers, certification, and so on.
- *Internal failure costs:* scrap, rework, lost time, returns, unused capacity, engineering changes.

■ *External failure costs:* returns, recalls, complaints, replacements, compensation, field service, repairs under warranty and under guarantee, product liabilities, and so on.

The total cost of nonconformance[3] is the sum of the four costs. It can reach as much as 20 percent of sales turnover for companies at an early stage of awareness. A hidden gold mine. By investing in prevention, the total cost of quality can be drastically reduced (Figure 7.5).

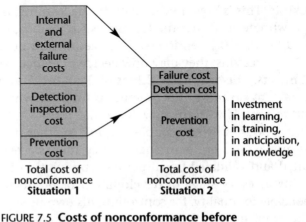

FIGURE 7.5 **Costs of nonconformance before and after investment in prevention**

The value of the investment in prevention can be explained with simple examples. Suppose that the cost of preventing the introduction of a defective resistor in a specific piece of equipment is arbitrarily 1 (cost of the inspection of raw material). If this resistor is soldered onto a circuit board, the cost of detection and repair may be 10 times greater (time spent diagnosing and correcting the problem). If the defect is identified at final inspection, the cost could again be multiplied by 10. When the item is in the hands of the user and breaks down, the cost to repair may well be 10 times greater again. Thus, by investing 1 in the cost of prevention, it is possible to decrease detection and failure costs by 1,000.

In conclusion, doing the thing right in the back stage is based on the principle of prevention. Everyone is responsible for understanding and controlling his own process, for keeping the learning in the form of standards, rules and procedures that have to be regularly updated.

Front-stage operations

How does process control apply to the front stage? Large sources of uncertainty appear on the fishbone diagrams governing each moment of truth.

FIGURE 7.6 **Fishbone diagram for a front-stage process**

Maintaining consistency of delivery depends on the stability and homogeneity of customers, a rather unpredictable "raw material." Their behavior and participation can evolve rapidly and unexpectedly during the service encounter. Employee behavior is another source of variation.

Screening of customers

Raw materials are inspected at the start of the manufacturing process according to precise standards. Similarly, customers walking into the front stage should be screened and prepared to ensure good control of the interaction.

This can be done through appropriate information or unambiguous signs. Certain activities are available only to club members; some restaurants accept men only if wearing a tie. Students are filtered with exams; patients in a hospital are physically and mentally prepared for the planned operation.

There are also customers who exhibit unacceptable behavior by making unreasonable demands (such as wanting to keep all their luggage with them in the airplane cabin), by being rude to employees or by otherwise breaking social norms (such as making too much noise or being drunk). Customers are not always right, and when they are not, prevention is better than cure. This can be done by screening at the point of entry (asking for proof of identity), by using information systems (to identify persistent offenders), by providing explanations and reminders (on safety rules or how to use the equipment properly) or even through economic sanctions (security deposits or contracts).

Governing behaviors and attitudes

The delivery process of a standard service is strictly defined, and customers' expectations are limited.

At a McDonald's restaurant, the interaction with frontline staff is controlled through detailed procedures and specific rules for product order and presentation, dress code and greeting manners. Customers have learned to restrict their demands.

McDonald's can therefore guarantee conformity and consistency. Some rules, such as the number of minutes after which an unsold hamburger must be thrown away, are mandatory and unequivocal, while others, like friendliness and courtesy, still remain "soft" and personal.

However, there is a limit to standardization. The dream of bureaucratic service organizations is to have customers who know exactly what to expect and employees with as little latitude as possible. Procedures are defined to cover every conceivable situation, and employees are trained to deliver mechanized, inflexible service. But customers do not appreciate being served by robots, and inevitably, as they interact, they put pressure on frontline personnel to be spontaneous and to provide more individual treatment.

At a call center, the main variables that control every interaction are either easily measurable (such as speed of answering and abandonment rate) or rather qualitative (such as accuracy and politeness). They are represented by a fishbone diagram in Figure 7.7.

To control qualitative variables, a quality controller or a team leader will listen to some calls to estimate the level of professionalism or the politeness of the answer. The objective is to give feedback and help the employee improve. But controlling the process means controlling people's behavior. Some employees may not appreciate this mode of supervision and may prefer trust and guidelines.

As the service gets more customized, rules become looser and take the form of protocols, principles or mottoes that guide work and explain the results that must be achieved. Service quality depends more on values, professionalism and skills than on hard-and-fast rules.

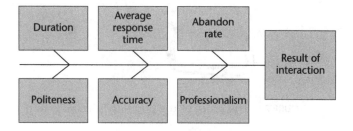

FIGURE 7.7 **Process control at a call center**

Guidelines, principles and goals, when communicated consistently, give frontline personnel more autonomy. For example, the Federal Express tagline "Absolutely, positively overnight" has often inspired employees to go the extra mile to serve their customers. At the Ritz-Carlton hotel, maxims and principles like "We are ladies and gentlemen, serving ladies and gentlemen" and "Ritz-Carlton hotels are places where the genuine care and comfort of our guests is our highest mission" are firmly rooted guidelines that create a strong and unique culture.

For quality control, prevention is the answer. When it comes to attitudes, behavior and professionalism, the solution is to invest heavily in the selection and training of staff and customers.

THE SECOND MOVEMENT: DOING THE RIGHT THING TO SATISFY THE CUSTOMER

The scene is set. Actors have learned their roles and will play their parts. Enter the customer. Value occurs at the intersection between delivery and perception, between the square of the script and the circle of the customer's requirements and expectations. The proof of the pudding is in the eating!

FIGURE 7.8 **The proof of the pudding is in the eating**

Perceptions are biased, fickle, colored by expectations and competitive offerings. How can frontliners manage to square the circle?

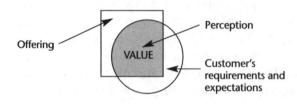

FIGURE 7.9 **Squaring the circle**

Customer satisfaction is expressed by the difference between perception and expectation. If perception exceeds expectation the value gap is positive, and the customer will probably be delighted.

Frontliners have three levers to manage customer satisfaction: do the right thing to maximize value, to influence perception, and to shape expectations.

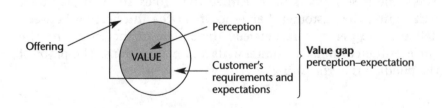

FIGURE 7.10 **Maximizing value, influencing perception and expectations**

Doing the right thing and customizing delivery

The right thing is what customers value. Part of what frontliners deliver may not be perceived by customers. This is the case, for example, with professors and lawyers when their message seems hopelessly esoteric. Professionals often focus on the technical aspects and forget the importance of explaining and giving the client an opportunity to learn and contribute. A well-known motto says "Fix the customer before you fix the problem!" Reassurance, empathy and responsiveness are essential elements of the relationship. Often companies lose customers because of lack of interest on the part of the employees.

Moreover, every customer feels unique, and customizing delivery is in the hands of frontline staff as long as they are supported by flexible processes. Employees should have enough freedom to own the relationship, bend the rules if circumstances demand it, break the mold and go an extra mile whenever they need to. They have to do the right thing on the spot and then report back to adjust standards and procedures if necessary.

Influencing perception

Perception is subjective, fickle, distorted by a number of biases. Impressions are filtered by an acquired pattern, a frame of reference, and shaped by experience. As the service experience remains intangible, customers need explanations in their own terms. They look for clues and tangible elements. They look for confirmation of their own opinions and tend to deny or discount what disturbs their beliefs. And when something goes wrong they blow it out of proportion and overgeneralize. A little detail could mar the whole picture. All impressions do not have the same importance. The first and the last impressions, the emotional and vivid moments, may color the whole experience.

Shaping expectations

Frontliners may try to clarify expectations and set the outline of the "contract" with customers through fair communication and achievable promises. A well-known rule is to underpromise and overdeliver. But expectations lie largely beyond their control. It is important that they have a good knowledge of the capabilities of the supporting processes and back-stage systems and that they make promises accordingly.

Measuring customer satisfaction

What customers value should be measured in customers' terms. Instead of measuring productivity of adjusters, Progressive Insurance measures the time from an automobile accident to the adjuster's arrival or the elapsed time from the accident until the claim has been paid.

A service quality index could summarize the results of key factors that may affect value. As customers add various impressions to form a final judgment, the overall satisfaction should be measured first. But a measurement instrument is useful only if it leads to action. It should therefore show how global satisfaction is created at each moment of truth. Vacation and tour operator Club Med measures satisfaction at different interaction points in each village along key dimensions such as quietness, cleanliness and comfort. This information makes up the "village barometer."

It is important not to try to guess what customers think but to have an external agency ask them or observe their behavior. Telephone surveys are popular, as they give a quick and fairly inexpensive response that is less biased than mail or comment cards. Many companies use mystery shoppers and focus groups as well.[iii]

In addition to direct measurement, customer complaints are another source of information, although dissatisfied customers are more likely to switch than complain. It is essential to actively seek out complaints, first to get feedback and improve, second to have a chance to recover the customers.

Recovery

Frontline staff must recover fast, because rework is visible. By reacting immediately they will prevent the memory of the incident from sticking. While customers are not always right, they calm down if they are listened to and a response is given promptly and effectively. The best

---

iii Eight to ten customers are gathered in a room and asked during in-depth interviews to comment about strengths and weaknesses of the service, important criteria for satisfaction, critical incidents and other factors.

course of action is to solve the problem at the source – the point where it arises – before it becomes a complaint. Although the person who receives a complaint may not always have the means or resources to solve it, he should be prepared to listen to the customer, give a clear explanation and ensure that corrective action is taken upstream by changing standards or preparing contingency plans. This is most often the responsibility of system designers and managers.

The Ritz-Carlton policy on this issue is as follows: any employee who receives a customer complaint "owns" the complaint. He is therefore responsible for calming the customer. He must react quickly to correct the problem immediately and to ensure that within twenty minutes the problem has truly been resolved. In fact, each employee is empowered to spend up to $2,000 in order to pacify an unhappy guest. An incident report form is then used to record and communicate customer dissatisfaction to those in charge of permanently solving the problem.

Value of customer (for the firm)

Customer satisfaction is a useful indicator as long as it leads to customer retention and loyalty. The correlation between satisfaction and loyalty is rather strong in businesses with high switching costs or proprietary technology, but tends to be less manifest in highly competitive environments.

The analogy of the "leaking bucket" explains the advantage of keeping a stable base of loyal, profitable customers, as it may be less expensive to retain them and reduce the leak than to get new ones.

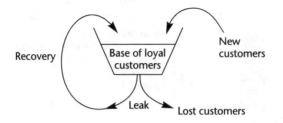

FIGURE 7.11 **Focusing on profitable customers**

Measuring satisfaction is a way to measure the leak, but given its limited resources the firm should focus on the most profitable customers. In some cases, it is possible to directly measure the leak by looking at the number of contracts terminated, equipment returned, credit cards canceled or accounts left inactive. When profitable defecting customers can be identified, special efforts may convince them to come back; in any case, these defectors may provide helpful feedback.

As Carl Sewell[4] explained:

> You don't want to deal with somebody just once; you want his business forever. We don't want to sell a customer just one car, but ten or twenty in coming years. ... If cars are $25,000 apiece, twelve cars cost $300,000. Then you have the parts and service work that go on top of it. It adds up to a substantial number, in our case $332,000. Every time you get a chance to sell a customer one item – whether it is a pack of gum or a car – you need to think about how much he represents in future business.

For British Airways, the "lifetime" value of a silver cardholder is about $120,000. Repeat business is the baseline profit, but economies of scope and cross-selling add to this. The longer customers stay, the more likely they are to buy more services. Furthermore, dealing with the same customers helps reduce the cost of relationship (operating as well as sales and marketing costs). Besides, such a stable customer base is a solid foundation for word-of-mouth communication, which is the most effective form of service advertising. Finally, a regular customer is less price-sensitive. Figure 7.12 gives a concise representation of the value of a loyal customer.

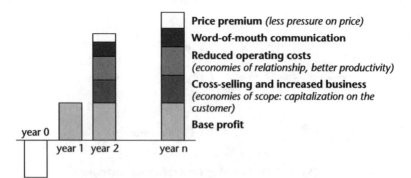

FIGURE 7.12 **Value of a loyal customer**

The "plus" of value and value re-creation

Doing the right thing right, or even rapid recovery when things go wrong, may not be sufficient to convince and retain customers. It may be necessary to provide the unexpected difference, the competitive edge that will delight rather than merely satisfy. An airline ticket is just an airline ticket. What makes the difference between one ticket and another one? Safety is an important factor, but fortunately all companies offer the same level of safety, because there are standards of safety in the industry. The answer lies in *secondary* but *determinant* aspects. Some are built at the design stage, such as frequency of flights and comfortable seats, but smiles, humor and responsiveness could make a difference as well. A small extra element may create a decisive advantage. For example, fun is taken very seriously at Southwest Airlines. Humor is at the top of the list of recruiting and hiring criteria. In the interview process, one request made of prospective employees is typically "Tell me how you have used humor to defuse a difficult situation."

Unfortunately, if a "plus" helps win market share, competitors will soon copy it or better it. Firms must continually create new differences and eventually re-create value. Even in a "bureaucratic" environment, frontline staff members often take the initiative to adapt the rules and bend the procedures. But the organization remains "bureaucratic" if the adjustments are limited and local and are not passed on to the system. There will be no learning, no progress.

Even if they are successful, organizations cannot rest on their laurels; they must continuously improve and re-create value. This leads to the third movement: a quality dynamic is set in motion.

THE THIRD MOVEMENT: THE DYNAMICS OF PROCESS ALIGNMENT

Survival in an open environment, under keen competitive pressure, requires never-ending adaptation to maximize the value perceived by customers in constant movement. To do the thing right the first time and to do better the second time, the organization has to get attuned to the voice of the customer. As the voice of the customer sweeps through the entire organization, from the front to the most hidden corners of the back, the sources of improvement become inexhaustible.

Everyone has to listen to the customer, a very demanding boss. But most companies pay lip service to the idea. They display posters or print laminated cards showing good resolutions like "Customers are our first priority" or "The customer is always right" or "We are customer focused." These rituals do not achieve much if they are not supported by a systematic and disciplined internal mobilization, an unending methodical journey to provide a seamless experience across all interactions and an alignment of key business processes across the whole organization from front to back. The challenge is to manage the tension between control and acceleration, between holding the gain and moving forward. In this context, continuous improvement is an established and accepted fact of life, a way to do things, a way to operate.

As the voice of the customer is deployed internally from department to department, from front stage to back stage, it is broken down at each and every internal customer–supplier interface along key business processes. The voice is transformed, filtered, materialized and quantified into specifications and standards at each interface. Each department, each unit is at the same time internal customer and supplier.

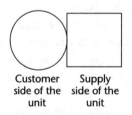

Customer   Supply
side of the   side of the
unit   unit

FIGURE 7.13 **Customer and supply side of a business unit**

Business processes are deployed along chains of customer–supplier relationships (Figure 7.14).

All business units, departments and functions have the unfortunate tendency to develop their own local culture and objectives, to think in terms of their own square, neglecting problems and demands outside their own "domain." They develop a local and vertical efficiency, according to a silo approach. By reconnecting the different units, breaking barriers and following key processes, it is possible to make malfunctions, waste, slack and non-added values visible.

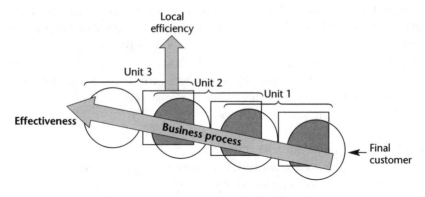

FIGURE 7.14 **Business process alignment**

Process improvement and reengineering

By drawing a map of a key process connecting different units, it is possible to make its purpose clearly visible to everyone. The *process owner* can then launch a dynamic of improvement and alignment. By reducing the distance and reconnecting internal suppliers and customers, adjustment is achieved on the basis of direct interaction. The *law of the situation* will teach each employee what to do. This is less binding than the *law of authority* imposed from above.

Four examples will show how this approach can bring efficiency and effectiveness, and help reduce the waste, the fat or the friction that has accumulated along processes. Generally speaking, the issue is the level of resources and staff time spent on activities that do not add value to the customer or to the firm.

First example: internal customer–supplier relationships

The first example considers an information technology department that produces hundreds of reports and documents for other internal departments. After the analysis of how many of these documents are actually read and used by internal customers, it may be discovered that half of them are never even looked at. The answer to the question "Why don't you ask users if they still find the information useful or if their requirements have changed?" will almost certainly be "I don't have time – I have to produce my 400 reports!"

The real problem is that internal and external needs change regularly under the pressure of new customer demands or the introduction of new technologies. Customer–supplier interactions must be regularly realigned to match these new needs, and ineffective documents, activities and habits (which are sometimes deeply ingrained) must be eliminated or corrected.

Value analysis is a simple yet effective technique to eliminate waste and inefficiencies or create new value. It consists of reviewing different activities by asking simple questions:

- Why do we carry out this activity?
- Does it contribute to satisfying customers' requirements?
- Is the benefit visible and understood by the customer?
- Does it contribute to business functions?
- Can it be eliminated?
- Does this activity help create a competitive advantage? Should it be developed further?
- How can it be improved, or substituted, to reduce cost or increase perceived value?

Second example: process improvement

The second example considers cross-functional processes that may cover several internal customer–supplier relationships and often include the final customer.

Figure 7.15 shows the processing of an insurance claim, which, in line with the principle of specialization and division of labor, has been broken down into seven activities.

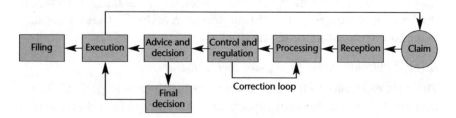

FIGURE 7.15 **Processing of an insurance claim**

Apparent on the flow chart are the usual stages:

- A unique process to deal with any type of claim.
- Errors and rework with a correction loop.

- Lack of communication between units and batch work leading to stock build-up and delays. The time needed to process the claim may extend to one or two weeks, although the actual work time on the claim itself may add up to just one hour.
- Waste and non-value-adding activities such as duplication and photocopying, moving, storing, filing, sorting, and checking and rechecking documents.
- Bad utilization of capacity and resources when demand is seasonal.
- Lack of flexibility and responsiveness due to centralized decision making and insufficient delegation.

The streamlining and realignment of this process reveal huge opportunities to cut time and waste and improve customer service. The method is simple and well known. What is missing is not intelligence, but commitment and resources. Under the guidance of a process owner, five key principles can work wonders:

- *Focus operations:* do not use the same process for dealing with all claims. Standard and simple claims can be handled by the customer at home, on the web. Other claims can be processed completely by the front-stage service representatives. Errors will be reduced through prevention by direct contact. Flexibility and responsiveness will be enhanced with delegation of signature. The original multistep process will be reserved for complex claims that need the attention of experts.
- *Do it right the first time:* if the job is done right at every step, the correction loop is no longer necessary.
- *Reduce waste and non-value-adding activities:* this can be done by regrouping operations, reducing batch size and automating some tasks.
- *Make better use of capacity and resources:* rebalance demand and capacity by introducing a flexible workforce and training personnel to become multiskilled and versatile.
- *Be more responsive:* make staff more aware of customers' needs and give them more leeway, reduce fragmentation, encourage teamwork and eliminate multiple approvals.

Third example: process redesign and reengineering

Often the introduction of new technology triggers a more ambitious improvement, a kind of "big bang" leading to the complete redesign of the process. "Big bang" does not mean that it is not possible to proceed step by step – caution must be exercised to avoid problems of implementation and resistance to change when the step is too high, as will be seen in Chapter 10.

This can be illustrated by the famous example given by Champy and Hammer[5] concerning financing requests at IBM Credit Corporation. The old flow chart shows the fragmentation and specialization of operations by function (Figure 7.16).

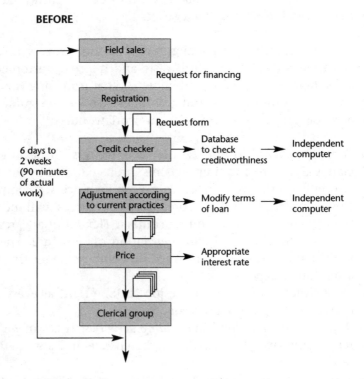

FIGURE 7.16 **Request for financing in IBM Credit Corporation**

The heavy use of information technology as well as the application of the five principles already mentioned made impressive gains possible. The cycle time was reduced to a few minutes for straightforward cases or a few hours for medium-hard cases, as shown in Figure 7.17.

The difficult task is to obtain good data and to show clear commitment by allocating proper resources for design and implementation.

It is a step-by-step approach:

- Select and define the process.
- Appoint a process owner and a project team.
- Benchmark existing systems and visualize the ideal system.
- Develop a new concept.
- Redesign the process.
- Sell the project and plan implementation (agreement, buy-in, negotiation).
- Test the new process in pilot sites.
- Implement across the organization.

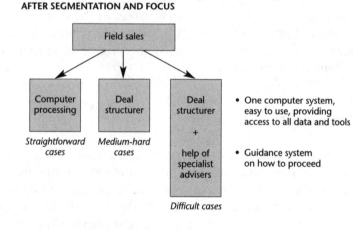

FIGURE 7.17 **Process redesign for credit request processing**

Fourth example: a seamless experience

Coherence and integration of experience should also consider the multiplicity of specialized contacts when the customer is passed from one service worker to another. The more contact points, the bigger the risk of fragmentation and dispersion. Coherence among employees can be established by coordinators, teamwork, job rotation, job enlargement and multiskilled employees.

A patient who spends a few days in a hospital may meet 50 people. How to make sense of all these contacts? At Boston's Beth Israel Hospital, a nurse is assigned to follow each patient's progress. The nurse is responsible for managing that person's hospital experience, from admission through to discharge or transfer to another unit of the hospital. The primary nurse, who is both caregiver and care manager, works closely with the patient's doctors and develops a 24-hour nursing-care plan for each assigned patient.

In other firms, customer account teams (sales, product groups, credit, customer and field service) are responsible for the overall relationship and present a single face to the customer. Teamwork and cooperation allow less direct supervision and leaner hierarchies. One way to achieve team cohesion is to use customer-centered measures. At a truck dealership, the sales, service and spare-part departments focus on their own particular tasks and seldom interact. By introducing a cost-per-mile solution for the customer and rewarding for revenues on sales, spare parts and service over the life of the truck investment, it is possible to align all noses in the same direction.

It is the same in the aircraft business with "wing-to-wing engine maintenance" (from the moment the engine is dismantled to the moment it is reinstalled).

CONCLUSION

The three movements of quality are essential to set up a dynamic of continuous improvement: doing the thing right, doing the right thing, and integrating processes and organizing a seamless experience. All three movements have to be connected by a systematic change process. It is all about implementation, as will be shown in Chapter 10.

Some organizations may start with product conformity; others may focus first on customer satisfaction or process reengineering. Whatever the approach, it is essential to have a common umbrella covering the three movements.

The drawback of the Six Sigma process is that it focuses primarily on zero defects and waste. The risk is losing momentum if the second movement – doing the right thing and developing competitive advantage – is not rapidly initiated to fuel the process.

8

BALANCING SUPPLY AND DEMAND

Another crucial and specific front-stage issue concerns the balance between supply and demand. Demand cannot be inventoried as the service is perishable, consumed at the moment of production. To make matters worse, the demand for a service often fluctuates widely – daily, weekly, monthly, yearly. The challenge then is to match the supply of services with a seasonal demand in an unstable environment. For example, when trading online, it can be observed that the hourly trading volume can be three times the average daily volume. But a spike in demand can be three times the average hourly volume. On a spiked day, the daily capacity should be multiplied by nine.

As Figure 8.1 shows, when demand falls short of capacity, the result is underutilization and idle capacity. When the level of demand enables optimum capacity utilization, the quality of service is good, queues are limited, and frontline staff are not under pressure. However, as demand increases beyond available capacity, quality drops and customers are held in queues or kept waiting by reservation systems. If demand rises still further, customers either have to come back at a less busy time or, more likely, are lost.

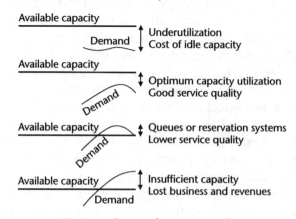

FIGURE 8.1 **Demand versus supply**

The definition of the best capacity level depends on the "cost" of underutilization – the cost of idle capacity and of loss of customer goodwill. For example, potential diners will be reluctant to walk into a restaurant that is almost empty, whereas a full dining room is convivial and reassuring. On the other hand, overutilization also has its costs in terms of lost business and the resentment of customers kept waiting.

MANAGING DEMAND

The starting point for the capacity decision is the demand forecast. Forecasting techniques, which use present and past experience to predict the future, fall into three broad categories: qualitative techniques, trend extension and explanatory methods.

Qualitative techniques are based on the opinions of customers or experts. The simplest procedure uses surveys in which relevant respondents are asked about their intentions for future behavior. Scenarios are used to generate coherent representations of the future as a function of certain eventualities. The analogy method requires finding a past situation similar to the one that is expected. The Delphi method, developed by Olaf Helmer and Norman Dalkey, involves surveying experts with a specific protocol.

The short- and medium-term future can be forecast by extending the past trend. The most basic approach is to plot a sequence of data and then simply extrapolate it. It may be useful to try to capture the basic trend of a time series by eliminating regular or seasonal variations and attenuating random variations. A moving average will bring out the trend from which seasonality can be extracted. The forecast is then obtained by multiplying the extrapolation of the trend by the seasonality factor. The seasonality of demand can be analyzed for different cycle durations: per day, per week, per month, per year.

Explanatory methods consider the evolution of demand as a dependent variable and link it to one or several independent variables. For example, demand for tennis courts depends on variables such as occupancy of local residences and hotels as well as weather conditions. The forecast is determined by the known evolution of the explanatory or independent variables, occupancy and weather.

Different methods can be combined. For example, how many courts should be built for a tennis club at a holiday resort? The first step is to find a correlation between court hours and guest nights, the evolution of which can be forecast. In that case, the best independent variable is guest nights at local hotels and private homes. The ratio of court usage to guest nights is obtained by a regression analysis over the past months. The calculation could give the following ratio:

$$\frac{\text{court hours}}{\text{guest nights}} = 0.05$$

The second step is to extrapolate the future level of guest nights by analyzing the time series over the past months or years and determining the trend and seasonality. The third step is simply to multiply the forecast of guest nights by 0.05 to find the demand for court hours and the required capacity.

Smoothing and scheduling demand

When demands for a service come from different sources, it may be important to deal with each of them separately. In the maintenance business, emergency calls and preventive action have different origins. Emergency calls are highly uncertain and random, whereas preventive action can be planned. There may be more emergency calls on some days of the week or at certain hours of the day, and so preventive maintenance can be scheduled to fill the gaps. Overall demand can be smoothed by combining the peaks and troughs of uncertain demand with planned and scheduled preventive action.

Similarly, seasonal patterns in the number of walk-in patients at a hospital can be smoothed out by scheduling appointments with patients staying at the hospital.

Influencing or shifting demand

When capacity is not sufficient to meet peaks in demand, privileged access and priority booking should be granted to frequent or loyal customers.

Although special off-peak offers may smooth out service utilization, old habits unfortunately die hard. Would it be possible to convince Mexicans to give up their daily siesta for the sake of improving traffic congestion at lunchtime? Hotels face a similar problem when they try to convince business travelers to stay on over the weekend, as do city councils when they try to convince drivers to avoid rush-hour traffic.

Demand can be shifted by offering a comparatively less attractive service package at peak times. The offer can also be reduced and standardized to speed up operations at peaks of activity, while incentives such as "no lines" or better service can induce customers to prefer slower times.

Pricing is the marketing mix factor most commonly used to influence demand. To succeed in changing customer behavior, prices must vary at different times and for different segments. There are many examples: weekend and night rates for long-distance telephone calls, off-season hotel rates, blue/green/red rates for electric power, varying highway tolls according to the hour.

Complementary or centralized demand

To increase off-peak utilization, complementary demand can be induced. For example, ski resorts can offer summer activities, restaurants, tea and bar service outside meal hours, hotels weekend packages and seaside resorts off-season conference packages for business groups.

Demand can also be smoothed by pooling resources, as in the case of a typing pool or a centralized call center.

Storing demand

Demand can be "stored" in a waiting line or a reservation system. Nobody likes delays, yet customers are often kept waiting on the phone or asked to line up at supermarket checkouts. Storing customers in a bar or lounge while they wait is a better solution than keeping them idle in a line.

With reservation systems, demand is redirected to available time slots, thereby smoothing capacity utilization and avoiding the need to keep customers waiting in line. Problems arise when customers make reservations, then do not show up. Faced with empty seats or empty rooms because of no-shows, airlines and hotels have adopted a strategy of overbooking. For example, a hotel may decide to overbook by three rooms. If only two guests do not show up, the hotel will not have enough rooms and will incur a cost: the cost of a room at a nearby hotel plus the loss of customer goodwill or loyalty. If four guests do not show up, one room will stay vacant and the hotel will incur an opportunity loss: the room contribution.

The overbooking decision should be based on a comparison between the cost of undercapacity (renting a room in a nearby hotel and customer dissatisfaction) and the cost of overcapacity (lost contribution). Overbooking is widely used by airlines, especially when it is relatively easy to shift passengers to the next flight.

MANAGING SUPPLY

When demand cannot be smoothed effectively, capacity should be made as flexible as possible. Flexibility is seriously limited by fixed investments and the existence of bottlenecks in a sequence of operations.

Analyzing the delivery process to look for bottlenecks

The simplified flow chart in Figure 8.2 shows patients arriving and being examined at Shouldice Hospital.

FIGURE 8.2 **Flow chart at Shouldice Hospital**

The arrival and service rate at the various stages must be well balanced to avoid lines and bottlenecks. Admission, examination, tests and dinner are all reasonably flexible and can be adjusted. The two main bottlenecks are the number of rooms available and the surgery's limited capacity (in terms of both facilities and available surgeons). Surgery capacity is a particularly acute issue for hospitals, since the length of an operation can vary greatly. Moreover, surgeons and anesthetists are not necessarily available at the same time. One way to optimize the use-capacity is to reduce the variability and segment the operating rooms into fast, medium-speed, slow and emergency rooms, according to the estimated duration of the operations.

Limiting the offer

Capacity can be increased by reducing the interaction time in a variety of ways:

- By simplifying the transaction: at peak times the menu is simplified; long and complex transactions are not accepted.
- By minimizing slack and wasted time between activities.
- By transferring some activities: a surgery patient may be anesthetized in a preparation room before entering the operating room and regain consciousness in a ward; nurses can leverage a physician's time by taking care of paperwork and preparing the patient for the visit.

Outsourcing activities

A more drastic way to increase capacity is to outsource noncore activities. By reducing kitchen activity in local restaurants and outsourcing food production to large centralized units, Taco Bell became more a food distributor than a restaurant. Smaller kitchens free more space for customers in the front stage, increasing available capacity and, ideally, turnover.

Using customer participation

Fast-food restaurants do not need waiters to bring food to the tables and clear them. The customer is a co-producer, expected to place his or her order, transport the food, clear the table – even eat faster at busy times. Hospital stays can be similarly shortened with patients' participation, if they accept that part of the cure will take place at home.

Developing capacity flexibility

The productive capacity of a service is constrained on one hand by the limits of the delivery system in terms of facilities and equipment, and on the other by the availability of labor. System limits can be expanded in several ways:

- *Varying the time available:* Changing the opening hours is the easiest way to modify capacity, as long as customers agree. For example, lighting tennis courts makes it possible to play at night; capacity is therefore increased. Similarly, the productive capacity of an aircraft doubles if it flies ten hours a day instead of five.
- *Flexible capacity:* The capacity of some services is elastic. By accepting standing passengers, trains and subways can double or treble their intake. Airlines cannot do this but can, by drawing a curtain, adjust the number of business-class seats. Venues such as sports stadiums and conference centers are often built to accommodate a variety of functions.
- *Sharing capacity:* Groups of hospitals may share heart treatment equipment or artificial kidney machines. Airlines can share airport gates, ramps and aircraft.
- *Renting equipment:* By renting conference rooms in hotels when organizing seminars, a conference center may avoid fixed investments.

A lack of staff reduces the available capacity, even if the physical capacity is adequate. There are several ways around this problem:

- *Scheduling work shifts:* When demand cannot be sufficiently smoothed, work shifts must be scheduled in line with demand forecasts. This is particularly important for firms such as telephone companies, hospitals, banks and fire departments. Scheduling operators is particularly complex when the service is available around the clock, seven days a week, and when employee preferences and constraints, such as maximizing consecutive days off, must be taken into account.
- *Using part-time employees or subcontracting personnel:* Part-time employees can be hired to supplement full-time staff. Fast-food restaurants, for instance, draw on a pool of college students. Fire brigades rely on groups of volunteers who train regularly and remain on call in exchange for a small retainer.
- *Sharing personnel:* Airlines sometimes share ground and flight personnel for secondary destinations; the employees simply wear different uniforms.
- *Ensuring that personnel are multiskilled and cross-trained:* When one operation is busy and another idle, employees can be reassigned provided that they are multiskilled. In the same way, they can be moved between the back and front stages at peak periods. At supermarkets, when checkout queues become longer, the employees in charge of stocking shelves can be called on to operate cash registers.

YIELD OR REVENUE MANAGEMENT

Computer technology advances and intense price competition among airlines have resulted in a new approach to maximizing revenue. This method, known as yield management, is aimed at increasing revenues by selling capacity to the right customers at the right time for the right price, using forecasting, segmentation and overbooking. With information technology, airlines can analyze an enormous amount of data in their reservation systems, understand past booking profiles and compare them with future trends. This enables them to adjust seat allocation on any flight according to fare levels, passenger demand and competitive pressure.

Yield management, also known as revenue management, does not apply only to airlines. It can be used by hotels, trains, cruise lines, car rental companies and electricity distributors. It is most appropriate for services that have a relatively fixed capacity with high fixed costs. In this case, the service provider may be tempted to offer a discount in order to better use the available capacity; market segmentation is often based on the sensitivity of customers to price and time of purchase.

Yield management maximizes revenue mainly through discount seat allocation and the level of overbooking.

Discount seat allocation

The simplest model considers two price classes (in fact, airlines offer several price classes): one for price-sensitive leisure customers and one for time-sensitive business travelers. Their demand curves are quite different (see Figure 8.3).

Leisure passengers plan their holidays and book in advance, whereas business travelers book late. The airline should avoid filling the plane too early with low-revenue traffic, and should set aside enough seats for late bookings. However, if too many seats are set aside and no late bookings materialize, these seats will be lost.

Airlines must determine the best yield by understanding and forecasting passenger booking demands for each flight. This is a difficult exercise, as the passenger mix may change from flight to flight, from day to day and from season to season. The balance between cheap seats and expensive seats is illustrated in Figure 8.4.

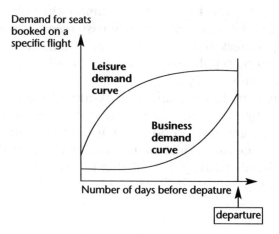

FIGURE 8.3 **Leisure and business demand**

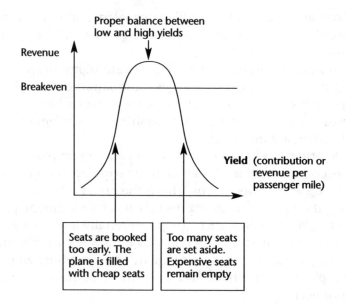

FIGURE 8.4 **Maximizing revenue**

Control of overbooking

Passengers who have booked a seat may cancel it or simply not show up at the time of departure. Airlines try to avoid flying with empty seats by overbooking, but they have to estimate the volume of no-shows on each flight and for each class of passengers. The efficiency of overbooking is measured by the number of passengers with no seat who have to be reimbursed or booked on the next available flight and given compensation.

Yield management has become a key competitive tool; it can increase revenue by 2 percent to 7 percent but can require support systems costing several million dollars. But such large investments are not always necessary. Yield or revenue management can be applied to the hotel industry, in which it is well established, and also to car rentals, passenger railways, media and broadcasting, and so on.[1]

MANAGING WAITING LINES

If demand and supply are still out of balance and there is no option to reserve in advance, customers have to wait in line, at the risk that some may leave and switch.

Waiting is part of everyday life. We are kept waiting at stores, stoplights and restaurants, or to get information on the phone; we line up for taxis, elevators and buses. Queues can be either physical or virtual – as when we are kept waiting by a telephone operator or placed on a standby list.

Waiting lines in the front stage can be compared with work in process in the factory. When there are sequences of operations, queues appear between operations. This is the case, for instance, at Shouldice Hospital (as shown in Figure 8.2) or at amusement parks such as Disney World, where each group is entertained while it waits.

In the front stage, an imbalance between supply and demand becomes highly visible as impatient and sometimes angry customers complain. In the back stage, all kinds of stocks can accumulate unnoticed.

The advantage of queues for the service provider is that they keep personnel busy and facilities and equipment fully utilized. But long waiting times are an obvious indicator that customers are not being properly served, and this negative impression can color their overall judgment of the service. The first impression and the first contact can deeply influence the rest of the experience.

Actually, a waiting line is a stock of customers. Just like an inventory, it is a symptom of a problem – like fever for a doctor. To cure the symptom it is necessary to find its root cause. This is the rational approach that focuses on operations and the match between arrival and service rates. Another approach considers the psychological aspect of waiting in a line. Depending on the context, a ten-minute wait can seem either no time at all or an eternity.

Operational aspects of waiting

Waiting line theory provides methods for calculating average waiting times when good information on arrival rates (demand) and service rates (supply) is available. As the rate of arrivals nears the service rate, the average length of the queue will quickly increase. This is why so many services operate best at around 75 percent of capacity.

Renault Minute, which performs instant car repairs, assumes a 75 percent utilization rate of facilities. Customers who do not want to wait have to pay a higher price to cover the cost of this idle capacity.

The first thing to do is analyze the delivery system to locate bottlenecks and queues at peak time. For example, in a bank branch with multiple tellers it is important to determine arrival rates and service rates at the various tellers during peak hours – Friday lunchtime, for example – in order to adjust supply and demand and identify the longest lines. Data are collected by recording arrival and service rates.

When the rate of arrival and the rate of service are highly random, the utilization of a facility can be obtained by calculating a simple ratio, the utilization factor:

Mean arrival rate: 3 customers per minute
Mean service rate: 4 customers per minute

Utilization factor of the facility: $\dfrac{\text{mean arrival rate}}{\text{mean service rate}} = \dfrac{3}{4} = 0.75$

The utilization factor obviously must be lower than 1 to avoid customer defection or costly overtime. The percentage of idle time in our example is $1 - 0.75 = 0.25 = 25\%$.

The average queue length is a function of the utilization factor, as represented in Figure 8.5.

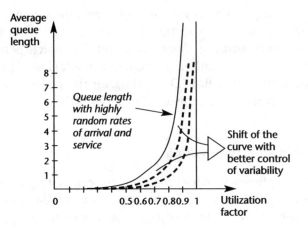

FIGURE 8.5 **Average queue length**

As the utilization factor approaches 1, the length of the queue tends to become infinite. The best way to reduce the length of the queue is to reduce the sources of variability (shift of the curve in Figure 8.5 and control of variability in Figure 8.6).

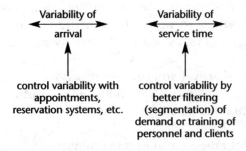

FIGURE 8.6 **Control of variability**

Waiting-line configurations

How many queues are needed? Where should they be located, and how should they be organized? There are basically two types of configurations for a service counter with multiple servers: multiple queues or a single queue (with the "take a number" variant) (Figure 8.7).

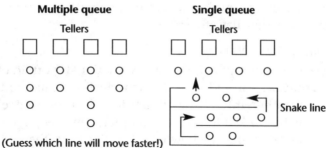

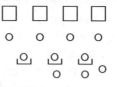

Customers with a number can sit down
and wait, or go out and come back later

FIGURE 8.7 **Waiting-line configurations**

- *Multiple queues open several possibilities:* You can create express lanes, as at a supermarket checkout. Division of labor is possible, the service can be differentiated, and customers can select a particular server. On the other hand, they will be anxious to choose the fastest lane and will resent having to wait behind a slow customer.
- *A single queue is perceived as fairer:* "First come, first served" is the rule. Reneging (or leaving the queue) is difficult, privacy is enhanced, and on average, customers spend less time waiting. However, service staff must be multiskilled.

Psychology of waiting[2]

The perception of waiting often differs from the objective time spent. Customer satisfaction is expressed by the difference between perception and expectation – two very subjective factors.

Acting on expectations

Expectations must be prepared so as to match the perception of the experience. It is better to overestimate than underestimate waiting time. To prepare customers for waiting, another contact mode can be

111

proposed (telephone, mail or a visit to another branch). Explanations will justify why they have to wait longer.

Taking cultural mindsets into account

In some cultures, jumping the queue is a national sport; in others, it is a serious offense. This indicates that fairness is an important aspect of queuing. Another interesting dimension is the distance between people, which is linked to the notion of territory. People stay at arm's length in some countries; elsewhere they flock together. Waiting can also have different meanings in different cultures.

Taking the perception of the experience into account

The customer usually goes through a series of interactions that lead to the final result. The first impression can deeply influence the rest of the transaction. For example, the sight of the waiting line may be more daunting than the actual waiting time. This is why, at Disney World, the length of queues is concealed by swerving lanes and partitions.

Taking the perception of the delivery process into account

People dislike empty time, so it is important to frame waiting pleasantly, with nice decor, quality furniture, flowers and music. Customers can be entertained by setting up mirrors or displaying magazines or by offering them a drink at the bar before dinner. To alleviate their anxiety it is essential to acknowledge their presence, tell them how long they have to wait and have a visible clock to make their perception of time more objective. It has been observed that customers' estimates of waiting time can be almost three times higher than actual, objective waiting time. Of two groups of customers, those kept waiting for more than a few minutes will judge the quality of service more harshly than those who wait less than half a minute.

CONCLUSION

For any service to work successfully, the crucial factors are the fit between the service mix and what key stakeholders value, and the fit between supply and demand. By now you should be convinced of the importance of the front-stage/back-stage concept, of the advantage of defining services by front-stage activities, and of the usefulness of the different tools and approaches developed so far. But it is not sufficient to have brilliant ideas and concepts. It is essential now to look at examples from industrial or professional services (Chapter 9), then to focus on implementation and understand how to put in place a successful change process (Chapter 10).

9

FROM INDUSTRIAL TO PROFESSIONAL SERVICES

It is about time to test the value and usefulness of the concepts and models developed so far. How do they apply at the two ends of the service continuum, from industrial services (back-stage and product intensive) to professional services (front-stage and relationship intensive)?

INDUSTRIAL SERVICES

There are not many ways to avoid the fate of commoditization and price pressure. Product innovation and performance superiority are one way to create a competitive advantage. Another is to develop services around the product.

To start with, services can be added to the product, which remains the key element of the transaction. This is the "product plus" approach. Customers may be willing to pay a higher price for additional benefits over the life cycle of the product. Next, the focus turns to the service itself. The customer understands its value and is willing to pay for it. But the price is still linked to the means and resources engaged, including the utilization of people, the time spent and the supply of spare parts.

Finally, the customer centers his attention on the outcome – the results achieved for him or his company. The price is linked to the expectation of future benefits.

Product plus

In the simple case of a water distribution company, the services offered around the core product are shown in the value creation cycle of

Figure 9.1. In front of each customer need, some possible elements of the service proposition are suggested within rectangles.

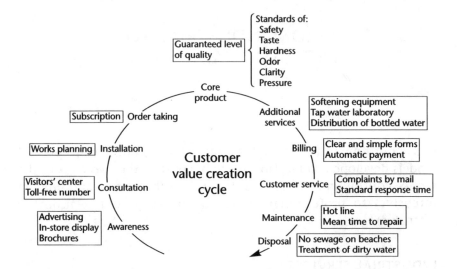

FIGURE 9.1 **Value creation cycle for water distribution**

Each element is chosen to optimize value for both the customer and the supplier, and to create a sustainable competitive edge. But is the customer willing to pay for the "plus"? There is a distinct risk that, over time, the service elements will be integrated into the product and become a legitimate accompaniment.

Medical oxygen, for example, is distributed in self-contained cylinders that optimize oxygen delivery, are easy to carry and simple to use, and include safety and maintenance instructions and a hotline number. These service elements are sufficiently visible, tangible and vital to justify a higher price than standard cylinders of oxygen.

General Electric's Medical Systems Division set up global facilities to allow constant remote diagnosis of its installed equipment. Devices inside the machines monitor performance and utilization. If they indicate that a piece of equipment is having a problem or reduced performance, a repair technician is dispatched before the hospital even knows something is amiss. Here, the service is invisible and intangible unless the machine breaks down. There is the risk that the service will become an inherent part of the product.

Product plus in a business-to-business environment

When SKF, the world's largest bearing manufacturer, decided to reorient the whole organization toward services, it created the Bearing Services Division with the objective of offering solutions to customers – selling products plus services.[1] Bearings are a vital component in all major industrial sectors, ranging from machinery and heavy industry to cars, trucks and railways. They appear whenever a part rotates. As more and more companies are able to make and sell bearings, they are now commodities.

SKF serves two markets: the before market (B2B) and the aftermarket. The before market is made up of original equipment manufacturers who buy large quantities and put a huge pressure on price. The traditional drive in this market is mass production, high quality standards and narrow margins. The aftermarket deals with replacement of bearings, and sales come largely through distributors. Availability and lead time are the main requirements.

As the company restructured itself around market relationships instead of manufacturing capacity, additional services provided before and after purchase enhanced its relationship with the original equipment manufacturer (see Figure 9.2). This led to the development of partnership and cooperation in areas from co-development at the design stage to manufacturing support in operations.

FIGURE 9.2 **Value creation cycle of an original equipment manufacturer**

The strength of the relationships was based on collaboration at all levels, extensive information and knowledge sharing, and eventually dedicated supplier equipment and staff on customer premises.

From unbundled services to full services

It may be more interesting to unbundle services from products and sell the service itself.

For example, Air Liquide supplies a number of services to accompany gas distribution: stock management and automatic resupply, monitoring of pipelines, delivery to the point of use, distant supervision of installations, maintenance of equipment, training and audits. These services can be sold separately, but in that case their price is based mainly on the resources they use, time per activity, utilization of people, salary costs and spare parts.

It may be more interesting to base the price on the results achieved for the customer. In the industrial aftermarket, the cost of bearings is minor compared with the cost of a standstill. Users seek to minimize downtime. For example, the priority for a paper mill is the recovery time after breakdown.

Again the value creation cycle is a useful instrument to show the needs of users in the aftermarket (see Figure 9.3).

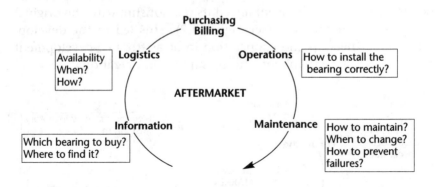

FIGURE 9.3 **Value creation cycle for aftermarket users**

SKF discovered that the industrial aftermarket had the same basic needs whatever the geographic region (see Figure 9.3). The lifetime of a bearing played a key role; it was affected by the quality of the product, how it was installed, protection from the environment and level of maintenance. Most of the downtime was spent locating the proper equipment or finding the right expert.

Figure 9.4 shows the elements of the service proposition that were provided by SKF Bearing Services through local maintenance support centers. Each country developed its own service strategy according to the local situation: creation of centers, joint ventures with local distributors, or agreements with industrial companies that had their own maintenance organizations.

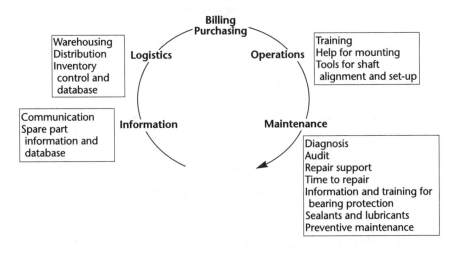

FIGURE 9.4 **Elements of the service proposition for the industrial aftermarket**

Full services are outcome based

When Rolls-Royce rents its engines to airline companies and is paid for every hour each motor is running, it provides a full service, from consulting and expertise to logistics, maintenance and training. Rolls-Royce has extended its front stage and installed teams of experts on the premises of airline companies and under the wings of their airplanes. It has taken full responsibility for doing the job of its clients on their value creation cycle. It is paid for the value it brings measured in the customer's terms, in hours of utilization. It gives customers what they want, what they value, rather than selling them only the products it makes.

The same approach applies to a diesel-engine company that sells not motors to purchasers of power plants for cities or factories, but kilowatt-hours.

With the "local customer support" concept, Air Liquide, through a seamless interface, takes care of all gas-related activities on customers'

117

sites in line with their requirements and under their control. These insourcing activities involve great human-resource support (logistics, maintenance, audits, accounting), require special tools and equipment, and abide by specific safety rules (see Figure 9.5).

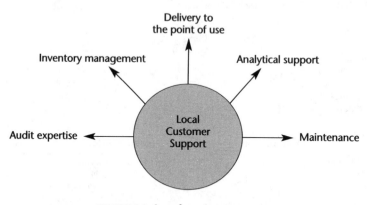

FIGURE 9.5 **Local customer support**

Service Master manages the cleaning needs of schools, hospitals, offices and industrial sites. With state-of-the-art equipment, technology and expertise, and by better organizing the job of its customers' staffs, Service Master can reduce costs, overheads and head count and improve quality.

The commitment of both parties is formalized in the contract, which lays out a concrete performance guarantee and limits of responsibility. Selling these types of services is an intensively planned act. It may take months and even years to sign a new service contract, and the signature is the point when the real work starts.

In summary, the move is from products to solutions

From product plus to full service, service reorientation is an opportunity to move from the red ocean of cutthroat competition to the blue ocean of relationship and cooperation.[2] That was the opinion of Jack Welch when he was CEO of General Electric:[3]

We might have scores of executives debating whether we would sell 50 or 58 gas turbines or several hundred aircraft engines a year, while we routinely handle the service opportunity of an installed base of 10,000 existing turbines and 900 jet engines.

To perform effectively, you need to look deep inside the business of the customer and be present on the customer's site with physical presence, electronic presence and mental presence. This is even more apparent at the other end of the spectrum in the sector of pure services, such as those offered by professionals.

PROFESSIONAL SERVICES

Professional services are essentially people businesses. They cover a vast range of activities, from advertising to legal work, to consulting. According to Mark Scott,[4] "All professional-service firms are united by one common characteristic – their assets walk out of the front door every evening and their livelihood is founded on fragile client relationships." This is clearly visible on the service triangle (Figure 9.6). Professionals are rather independent and can easily cut their links to the firm. Clients that have a strong relationship with their professionals may follow them. But the firm may retain them with a solid brand and reputation.

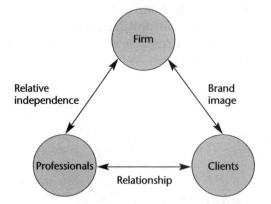

FIGURE 9.6 **The service triangle for professional services**

The firm has to win the most interesting clients and projects, and attract and keep the best professionals. But managing a good balance among the protagonists and doing well at the three corners of the triangle proves to be a difficult exercise. Talented professionals with knowledge enjoy a technical superiority and relative independence vis-à-vis the firm and the clients. They tend to relate more to their peers and professional associations than to the firm. They have money and prestige. What they need most is interest in the job, challenge, fun and freedom.

The balance between the need to regulate and manage professionals' activities and their need for independence is especially difficult to achieve, and managerial jobs are often temporary roles. Leadership is best exercised by managers with proven professional expertise who negotiate a consensus on values and methods.

On the other hand, clients expect a personal relationship and reassurance, explanations given in terms they understand and not in a cryptic language.

Two examples of professional-service firms will further show the relevance of service concepts and instruments developed so far.

Consultancies

The service-intensity matrix is a useful tool to analyze the positioning of consulting firms.

In the top left corner of the matrix, strategy consulting firms such as McKinsey and the Boston Consulting Group provide state-of-the-art, extended solutions. Clients expect deep involvement, risk sharing and bottom-line results.

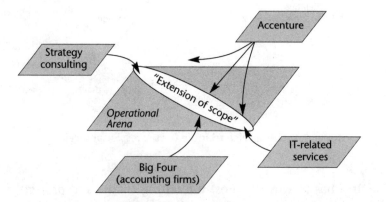

FIGURE 9.7 **Positioning consulting and accounting firms**

At the bottom right corner, IT-related services such as EDS, Cap Gemini, software vendors and system integrators provide more routine applications, which become even more price sensitive as they become more popular and commoditized. To avoid being cornered in this uncomfortable position, they tend to develop the consulting aspect of their engagements and move up the diagonal – the value chain – toward more integrated business solutions.

The Big Four accounting firms (Ernst & Young, Pricewaterhouse-Coopers, KPMG, Deloitte) have the same problem. They strive to move to consulting, which provides better fees with the risk of being judge and party. Firms such as Accenture tend to cover a large scope of activities along the diagonal, from business process management to systems integration to business integration, linking technology, operations, structure and strategy.

The vocation of consultants such as McKinsey is the transformation of organizations and the management of the change process. As they enter their clients' boardrooms, they have to commit to results and eventually share risks. Clients expect strong involvement, good coordination with the engagement team and joint problem solving. This highly interactive teamwork is mainly in the front stage. The service content is quite high. It is important to avoid the natural slide of solutions and applications down the diagonal toward commoditization (see Figure 9.8).

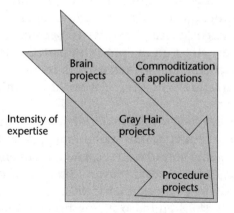

FIGURE 9.8 **Commoditization of consulting services**

Systems integrators, on the other hand, provide network services and application programs that are integrated with other products in their back stage. Front-stage activity is focused on the distribution and implementation of applications.

The service mix

It appears that professionals can charge *higher rates* if they get better clients and better projects, not more clients and more projects. By narrowing their customer base and targeting fewer key clients with whom they develop deep and long-term relationships at the strategic level, consultancies can focus on results and develop value-based pricing schemes. Instead of charging for the activities performed, they charge for the actual transformation of clients. They can simultaneously reduce marketing and operating costs and better utilize their labor force. And when clients are multinational companies, worldwide coverage becomes a significant competitive advantage.

At the operational level, another key success factor is the *leverage of professional time*. Leverage results from the division of tasks among partners, managers and consultants. Partners and "rainmakers" should not do tasks that can be done by managers or consultants. Doctors should not do tasks that can be done by nurses or administrative assistants. Leverage can be measured by the ratio of partners to managers and managers to consultants (in the simple case of an organization with three tiers). In a firm like Accenture, the leverage ratios for one partner are 1:6:30; in a traditional law firm, the ratios could be 1:2:5. There is a clear incentive to become a partner, as the leverage has a direct effect on the profit for partners. In addition, the billable time for partners and managers is reduced as they spend more time on marketing activities, relationships with clients, coaching and mentoring.

Recruitment and *selection* of talented individuals is the most important factor affecting results, teamwork and the quality of relationship with the client. Leading consultancies spend a lot of energy recruiting top brains, results-oriented team players. *Training* of professionals is closely related: training in content (analytical tools or industry knowledge), in teamwork skills and also in the firm's values, policies and processes. The most important asset of professional firms is knowledge; they have to manage it, share it and distribute it at high speed and with great efficiency.

As David Maister[5] explains, "Professional firms should stop thinking about billable and nonbillable hours, and start thinking about three new categories: income time (serving clients), investment time (creating one's future) and individual time (everything else)." Investment time, in particular, should focus on knowledge management.

Finally, this sophisticated and talented workforce should be developed and maintained with a *management style* and a *culture* that will enhance commitment and enthusiasm through mentoring and coaching by partners and managers, care in assigning adequate challenges to consultants to help them gain experience, fair compensation and promotion. The firm's culture plays a major role in homogenizing behaviors to deliver a consistent quality level. The culture is encoded in strong values, summarized in mottoes such as "Care, share, dare."

Financial services and retail brokerage

Deregulation, information technology and the web expansion made it more and more difficult for full-service brokerage firms to ignore the threat of discount and online brokers. Full-service firms charge high commissions as they offer investment advice in return.

The first wave of discount brokers was led by Charles Schwab, which ventured out boldly with the ambition of providing investors with suitable access to securities trading. It embraced technology to pursue a multichannel strategy that included branch offices, telephone-based brokerage services and online trading to serve customers' need for convenience. Branches focused on opening accounts and assisting customers with important transactions. The automated telebroker phone service enabled customers to make trades, check account status and get quotes without talking to a customer service representative.

With the sudden appearance of a number of websites that enabled clients to buy and sell stocks online for a fraction of what full-service brokerages charged, the basic trading job was turned into a commodity. Charles Schwab moved quickly to e-business and merged discount brokerage with online brokerage, giving phone and branch representatives web access and training.

This dramatic evolution is illustrated on the service-intensity matrix in Figure 9.9.

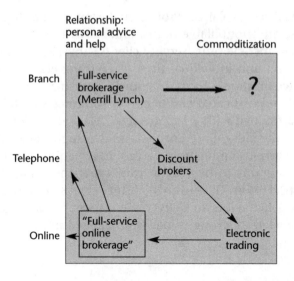

FIGURE 9.9 **Positioning of stockbroking firms**

As firms slid down into the bottom right corner of the matrix, their business became commoditized with considerable pressure to reduce commissions. To survive as a broker it was essential to learn how to use the technology, market a wider array of products and offer customers real value-added services in the form of advice and judgment.

As the brokerage business deals mainly with bits of information that can be easily processed and distributed, it was possible to enrich and personalize the relationship, and provide the client with advice and help, at little additional cost. Charles Schwab repositioned itself as a full-service online broker educating customers and empowering them with tools for asset allocation, stock selection, financial planning, access to information and perspective, so they could do the job themselves. The next step was to enter Merrill Lynch's territory by reinventing full service, blending internet-based trading with some of the investment advice offered by full brokerage firms. Charles Schwab introduced a series of specialized services for active investors with substantial portfolios. With a higher tier account, the client could have access to brokers and personalized investment advice.

As Charles Schwab was taking steps to enter the full-service brokerage market, Merrill Lynch responded by offering internet trading, positioning itself as a one-stop source for financial services. It provided a continuum of products and options for self-directed investors as well as full-service delegators.

The slump in the equity market in 2000 exposed the effects of Merrill Lynch's overexpansion and poor cost control and prompted a serious overhaul of the group. The system was jammed by a large number of small accounts that financial advisers could not service properly. Segmentation of the customer base was a compelling necessity. On average, financial advisers handled 550 accounts each, a number that was too large for clients to be served in a consistent way. By reducing this number to 200, the firm could offer the "ultimate client experience" with more frequent contact, rapid response to problems and attention to details. The Supernova project[6] successfully implemented a 12-4-2 approach, prescribing the minimum number of contacts to be proposed to each adviser's 200 primary clients: 12 monthly proactive contacts, of which four were portfolio reviews and two face-to-face meetings.

A rather controversial move was to transfer the 350 remaining accounts to the Financial Advisory Center, a centralized call center. These smaller accounts were to be called systematically at least four times a year to ensure that their needs were being met.

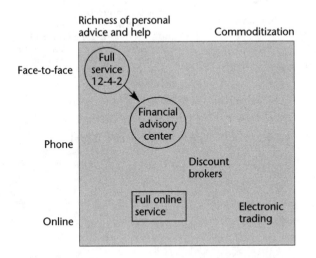

FIGURE 9.10 **Segmentation of Merrill Lynch customer base**

Figure 9.10 shows the position of the two segments that replaced the wider original target. The clear advantage of dealing with more homogeneous segments is the ability to streamline processes. Two well-focused processes on each segment are more effective than a unique process that fits all customers.

For the Supernova approach to succeed, financial advisers needed to be convinced to change their operating style from "hunter" to "farmer." They had to take a more systematic approach to dealing with their clients and work more closely with assistants who would filter calls, prepare and update folders, and organize appointments. This important cultural reform had to be carefully implemented through a change process that will be described in the next chapter.

The leaking bucket model can further explain what is at stake.

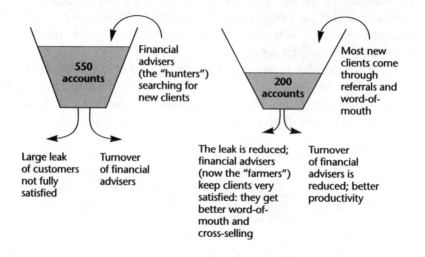

FIGURE 9.11 **The leaking bucket model**

10

MANAGING THE CHANGE PROCESS

The market power is in value. Value leads to results. Managers have to continually ask themselves how to inject more value and reduce costs to avoid the lethal spiral of commoditization, overcapacity and price war. With strategic repositioning, new segmentation and new service propositions, they re-create value to move the organization out of the troubled seas of intense competition to calmer waters or to a niche harbor. Tools such as the service-intensity matrix and the value creation cycle are useful in this quest for a solid and sustainable superiority.

Moreover, managers have to set in motion or rekindle a dynamic of continuous improvement to reduce quality gaps, use capacity more fully and find opportunities for differentiation at a faster pace than the competition. The dilemma is to manage the tension between continuity and change, between control and acceleration, by making the customer, this very demanding boss, more present in everyone's job. This continuous improvement fits together the three movements of quality along key processes that run through the organization and link the back stage to the front stage.

Processes are like beams: they tend to rust, bend or break. The objective is to avoid natural decay, to do right the first time and better the second time, to cut the waste and realign processes. Continuous improvement has no limit, because it concerns everyone and every process, and the possibilities to create competitive differences are infinite (see Figure 10.1).

Turnaround, repositioning and realignment look achievable in theory, but most firms do not perform well when it comes to practice and implementation. Change strategists often meet in exotic resorts and come out with grand new answers. Change recipients, on the other hand, are not as excited as their managers would expect. Regularly swamped with waves of new change programs with evocative titles, they tend to develop an immune-defense response. For example, the continuous improvement approach, the overall umbrella that covers the three movements of quality, reappears regularly under a new name, stressing a different aspect: Total Quality Control, Total Quality Management, Kaizen, Business Process Reengineering, Time-Based Management, Six Sigma, Lean Six Sigma, Change Acceleration Process and so on.

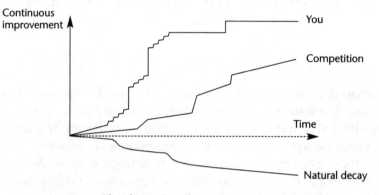

FIGURE 10.1 **The dynamics of continuous improvement**

Often the initial excitement does not last – because of a lack of persistence; a change of focus; too much pressure; an overly fast initiation, followed by burnout; a promotion of the person in charge; or simply a low level of motivation and resistance to change (Figure 10.2).

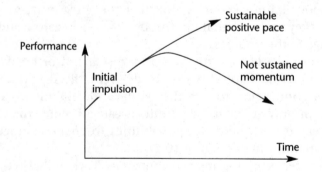

FIGURE 10.2 **Performance after initial impulsion**

What is missing is not vision, concepts and theory, but method and persistence. Change does not just happen. It must be guided by a systematic process that focuses on implementation and action, a systematic method for leveraging innovation and refurbishing the organization, a framework for cultural change.

A SIMPLE ANALOGY

A good way to illustrate the various aspects of the change process is to consider the simple analogy of a person trying to lose weight.

Sticking to a diet requires a systematic approach. First, you have to understand that you have to move out of the comfort zone of old habits. There are many reasons to postpone the diet in the rush of daily life. You do not change when someone tells you you should. You change when you tell yourself you must. Most often, it is only a sense of crisis, a threat to your health that establishes the right level of urgency. You may then need the advice and support of your family, friends or doctor. On the other hand, the advantages of the new perspective will give you the courage to get started and to devise a plan of action.

This preparation phase revolves around four questions:

Why move?
Who is going to help?
What is good about the new perspective?
How do I get there?

The implementation phase is about action. Once your first attempts have been successful, you must stick to your new habits and practice them on a regular basis. At this stage you may need regular reviews and visible measurement of the progress made. Finally, you establish the new rules and behaviors as normal practice. You hold the gain.

Action occurs in three stages:

Experiment and learn. The first wins.
Deploy and keep momentum.
Consolidate. Set the rules. Maintain the gains.

The same questions and stages are found when a change process is implemented in an organization.

THE FOUR QUESTIONS

Why? Establishing a sense of urgency

Are enough people dissatisfied with the present situation, and do they understand the need to move out of the comfort zone?

Like a carriage that regularly travels the same road, we sink deeper and deeper into our habits, into the same rut, the same groove. After years of repetition, regular practices turn into routines, traditions or even doctrines. In the comfort zone, entrenched in our habits, we cling to the status quo, we ignore negative signals, we seek confirmation and reinforcement of our beliefs, and we discount the future. So, before deciding to pull the carriage out of the rut onto a new and uncertain track, there must be a serious source of dissatisfaction; we must feel a sense of urgency. Most often, people do not change when they are told there is a better option. They change when they have no other option!

This analogy applies well to an organization. The first condition for change is dissatisfaction with the existing situation. More often than not, it takes a crisis to shake up the organization, dismantle vested interests and generate the burning need to move out of the comfort zone. After crossing the Rubicon River, Julius Caesar ordered his troops to burn all the boats to cut off the escape route and the possibility of a pullback. There was nothing left for the soldiers to do but advance and conquer.

In a turnaround, everyone will recognize the necessity to change and find a new path. The situation teaches people. The desire to survive is greater than the anxiety over moving and learning. But when the firm is still doing well and needs only a realignment, it may take a lot of management energy to convince employees that change is necessary.

Enlightened managers may anticipate the crisis and raise awareness of the need for realignment by dramatizing the situation and painting a harsh picture. They can point out the mounting threats, the real situation or the gold-mine opportunity.

Threatened by dozens of online brokerage sites that were turning the basic business into a commodity, Merrill Lynch understood the severity of the threat and repositioned its service proposition to better satisfy clients' needs and offer them real value.

Teaching and convincing people can become an exhausting task unless symptoms and problems are made visible and patent. This can be done by comparing the firm with competitors or by benchmarking similar processes in different industries.

Measuring tangible and explicit indicators, such as waste, non-value-adding activities, stock, lost time, and customer satisfaction and loyalty, can bring reality and objectivity. Another mode of persuasion is to reintroduce the voice of customers who are not fully satisfied, as well as the opinion of noncustomers.

In any case, a clear diagnosis supported by facts, results and comparisons will wake up the organization. Moreover, top management can express its determination by sending out strong and loud signals in the form of major structural changes, plans for layoffs or drastic cuts in budgets.

When the chief executive officer of SKF decided to change the strategic orientation of the firm from a traditional product line to a market approach, he realized that the entire culture of the company needed a jolt. He took a bold step: he elevated the status of sales teams dealing with the aftermarket to the same level as the manufacturing companies themselves. The creation of the Bearing Services Division was a prominent indicator of the need to develop a new service culture.

Who? A steering committee and a guiding coalition

Who is going to help develop the new vision and, more important, organize and guide practice? The guiding coalition can take the form of a steering committee, an executive council, a national implementation team, a process improvement office or a center of expertise. Whatever its name, its role is to lead and pilot the change process.

The first task is to help establish the new strategic intent and build commitment and passion for it. The next step is to analyze the political landscape to find out who the principal players are, what their source of power is, what the main constraints and obstacles are, and where to start to have the best chances of success.

At the implementation stage, the steering committee will help communicate and teach the new vision. It will organize review sessions and robust dialogue that should end with clear commitment and accountability. Performers are to be rewarded, and nonperformers have to be trained and mobilized.

Finally, as the new culture becomes established the steering committee will set the new rules, the new standards, the new performance measurement systems that will consolidate new habits and behaviors.

What? Developing a convincing new vision

It is risky to unfreeze the organization and get people out of their comfort zone without offering them a convincing new vision, a vision they will share.

Where is the promised land? The Hebrews were ready to leave their lives in slavery when Moses promised them a land of milk and honey, a metaphor for food every day and a little luxury from time to time. His promise was imprecise but convincing. In fact, he did not deliver milk and honey but helped them build a nation.

The vision should provide meaning and excitement and help everyone understand the "why" as well as the "what" of his or her job. Everyone will be able to internalize strategic directions and understand the importance of weaving and reweaving the fabric of cooperation across units. Energy is mobilized in the right directions, and resources are allocated to projects linked to strategic priorities.

The most challenging task is to lead, that is, to show commitment and constancy of purpose but to remain flexible enough to unleash energy and participation. The road map is lightly filled in to give room to maneuver. Guiding implementation and practice requires pedagogy, flexibility and respect for local situations, even more so when dealing with the service aspect in the front stage.

To sell the business mission inside the organization, it is very relevant to use a strong theme, one that is easy to grasp, easy to communicate and easy to remember. For example, the mission statement used at SKF was "We are in the business of trouble-free operations." The customer does not care about the type of bearing or the model number, but is concerned to have the machine operating with the highest availability.

The "what" is essential to give goals and directions. The next question is how to get there.

How? Analyzing the situation – how to get there?

Once the sense of urgency gains acceptance and the new vision is established, the next imperative is to draw up the battle plan and plot the route. Change is a messy process at the beginning. Harvard's Clayton Christensen has demonstrated through his research that innovative products and services hardly ever work when they are first released.[1]

To limit the level of confusion and immune-defense reactions, the implementation should proceed step by step. Early experiments and successes will serve as bellwether projects that will endow the movement with a certain amount of credibility and establish bridgeheads.

These projects should be significant and cross-functional (across functions or aligning back stage and front stage). The initial effort should focus on the parts of the system where there are the most possibilities.

Choosing the right people and the right teams may be more important than deciding on the content of the project, as it is important to remain flexible and respect local situations, especially when the service aspect dominates.

The best way to understand how to proceed is to refer to the diffusion model (Figure 10.3). Innovators will prime the change movement, as they are the adventurous ones who are motivated to take up the challenge. They will be chosen for their motivation and their competence, but they need room to experiment and maneuver, ownership of the project and resources (mainly time).

The early adopters are a slightly larger group won over by the innovators. The ones to target are the opinion leaders – the respected people with influence, the gatekeepers who control important resources and local managers in the front stage. Then comes the big pack of followers who will adopt the new approach only when they see visible and tangible results.

Finally the laggards or resisters may feel no sense of urgency and may deny any reason to change.

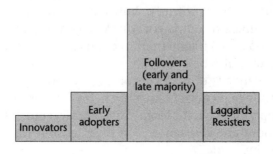

FIGURE 10.3 **The diffusion model**

The difficult part is to manage the transition from one group to the next to get the right momentum. Some people matter more than others, as they bring energy and knowledge and are able to persuade people around them.

THE THREE STAGES OF IMPLEMENTATION

The preparation phase draws to a close with the answer to the four questions: why? who? what? how? The action and implementation phase advances in three stages.

At the *initiation stage*, a few champions will prime the process with pilot experiments. To give it momentum, a number of opinion leaders should follow suit. The role of management at this stage is to create the right climate, protect the innovators and allocate resources and time to them.

At the *deployment stage*, early adopters and opinion leaders will play an important role in translating the new ideas into practical terms and diffusing them to the majority of followers and late accepters who prefer to wait and see. These people need tangible evidence and exposure to specific projects or results before becoming confident enough to commit. At this point, management has to apply the right level of stretch, define more clear objectives, introduce measurement and accountability, and align performance and reward.

Finally, at the *consolidation stage*, behaviors are aligned in the same direction as new rules and values consolidate the new culture.

Stumbling blocks and obstacles are generally easy to identify. They often originate from turf battles between established silos or strongholds, paralysis caused by intrusive bureaucracy and systems that have become too complex or outdated. A lack of communication between departments, too much fragmentation or an excessive number of hierarchical levels may also be in play.

The real challenge is to find the courage to address these problems and lead the change process. Leadership here means enabling the right people and applying the right level of tension. Too much tension leads to stress, burnout and resistance. Too little tension leads to complacency and apathy.

Leadership also means walking the walk and setting up the right climate to release people's energy. Then the animating style is progressively replaced by a programming style, a more top-down approach that establishes new values, new rules and measurement systems.

The initiation stage – experiment and learn: the first wins

Practice starts with pilot experiments to test and adjust the new approach. The new path must be traced and established rapidly with visible activities and projects. The change process has to remain flexible and evolutionary as things take shape step by step, in unknown territory. It is not possible to move the whole organization at once; the steering committee should look for the parts of the system with the most potential to show rapid results. It has to find and select the key players, the innovators, the champions who are willing and able to take the challenge, who have a high level of motivation and passion for the concept. At this stage, who should do the job may matter more than what should be done.

The first projects should be significant and cross-functional but not too vast to be completed within a reasonable time period. They establish strong pockets of innovators and credible bridgeheads that get management's attention and peers' interest.

Four multiplicative factors are at play in the conversion of attempts into successful stories (Figure 10.4). They may offset each other. Champions' and project teams' motivation and dedication may compensate for a lower level of competence or experience. A high level of challenge increases the credibility of the experiment, but the associated risk should be offset by a helpful context. If the context is not favorable, failure is probable. I may be motivated to play the piano, I may know how to play, and I may choose the right music and a good level of difficulty, but if I do not have a piano to play on and the free time to practice, I will not succeed.

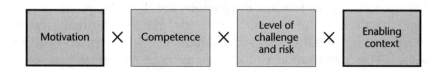

FIGURE 10.4 **Four factors at play in the conversion of attempts**

The job of the steering committee is to protect the experiment, empower the team and give it the proper resources and, more precisely, time. Experience shows that a full-time assignment to the project is a key success factor. Day-to-day activities and long-term investment in the change process should be clearly separated.

These projects will be carefully watched by the rest of the organization, and particularly by opinion leaders, local managers in the front stage and gatekeepers, people with influence or with control of important resources. Some will watch, analyze and follow suit. These early adopters are essential for the diffusion of the movement, as they will help translate the experiment into something the rest of the organization can understand. They are in a good position to communicate and actively advocate the change approach and convert a number of followers. Word of mouth is the best form of communication at this early stage, and the role of middle and local managers should not be underestimated. People change when they notice that others like themselves have changed and flourished. The steering committee will watch over this translation, assimilation and diffusion to prepare for the next stage.

The deployment stage

Once the movement has been primed, it begins to spread inside the organization, but now the change process is better understood and communication becomes essential. People have to be taught about the situation, the urgency of change and the new vision. A strong theme that is easy to grasp and easy to memorize will raise awareness and interest. For example, messages like "Make SKF easy to do business with" or "We are in the business of trouble-free operation" are simple enough to stick in the mind.

Public statements, charters, exhortations, poster campaigns, slogans, newsletters, lectures and parables are all useful, provided they meet practice. On their own, they are no more than ritual incantations. An organization cannot be changed by proclamation or by decree. The organization will change as more and more people are convinced to try and as attempts are converted into success stories. Again, the same four factors are involved, but not in the same way (Figure 10.5).

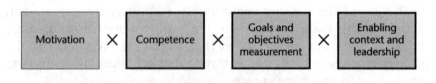

FIGURE 10.5 **Reconsidering the four factors at play**

Motivation

Why should I try a new way of doing things? What's in it for me? Employees may see the pain and not the gain. Do they get better control and more significant tasks? What is the advantage of unlearning and relearning? Do they feel able to cope? Do they lose prestige and power? But above all what is the compensation, the reward? Is there a possibility of promotion? As the motivation of frontline employees may differ from that of the back-stage people and as the motivation factor gets more complex to manage and develop, other factors may compensate for it.

Competence

Training may increase self-confidence, sense of control and willingness to try new things. It should be linked to action to establish new behaviors, ideally through long periods of immersion to experiment with the new practice and participate in its definition.

Goals and objectives

As the situation gets better defined and the results better measured, goals and objectives can be assigned and performance appraised. Measurement is essential to define objectives and see progress. What gets measured gets done. The most valid indicators are not financial assessment and results. These indicators are lagging. The focus should be on underlying and tangible indicators directly linked to the process, such as wasted time, delays, wasted capacity, stocks, number of defects, rework, overhead, non-value-adding activities, cycle time, value creation, perceived pluses, customer satisfaction or loyalty, and so on. The right level of stretch will depend on the competence of the project leader and his team. A challenge superior to competence leads to anxiety. A challenge inferior to competence leads to boredom.

One of the major risks is wasting resources through a surfeit of ideas and projects. It is essential to coordinate and channel the change process by linking it to the big picture, to the strategic directions. The steering committee will determine the speed and pace of change by reviewing projects, setting priorities and allocating resources. It will encourage transfer, sharing, cross-fertilization and adaptation of best ideas and practices across demarcations and boundaries.

Enabling context and leadership in a climate of trust

Employees are entitled to experiment without worrying about failure. Obstacles to empowerment – too many layers of hierarchy, bureaucracy, cross-border and territory feuds – have to be considered and eventually modified or removed. The context has to be such that listening and experimenting are in the employees' interest. Empowerment leads to accountability, feedback and recognition. Rewards and recognition need to be aligned with performance.

Communication is linked to results and comparative data. Peer pressure is a powerful way to convince people to change. Who would want to lag behind or get worse results than his or her colleagues?

Values and behaviors are reinforced when employees see who does not get promoted, who is retired early, who is cut out of the loop. Allocation of time and resources is also a clear indication of management priorities.

Managers show their commitment not only by repeating over and over again the same message but also by paying regular visits and practicing what they preach. As the saying goes, "People learn more from observation than conversation."

As the change process is deployed, it gradually shifts from a "pull" mode to a "push" mode. After involving people and selling the concept, it is time to tell late followers and resisters the new values, the new rules, the new appraisal and reward systems.

What should be done with resisters? Their possible conversion may bring more momentum to the process, but their denial of the need to change and their opposition may be too corrosive. In the latter case, they will have to be neutralized or removed. Ideally, their conversion is facilitated at this stage by the accumulation of objective facts and results, clear expectations of performance and peer pressure.

The consolidation and alignment stage

The ultimate objective is for the new practices to become second nature, the normal way of doing business.

Culture is shared basic assumptions, values and rules that have been learned and distilled through practice. The organization should now be "refrozen" around the new norms, operating procedures and systems to hold the learning. The new systems must be institutionalized for change to be sustainable and continue forging ahead.

What happens to the four factors at this consolidation stage?

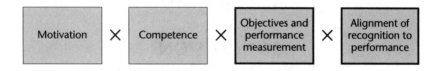

FIGURE 10.6 **Consolidation factors**

The emphasis now moves to performance measurement and recognition. Actors align their behaviors according to the new resources and constraints established by the new assessment systems. On a soccer team, when forwards are assessed only on the number of goals they score, it is to their benefit to score, but not necessarily to help their partners. If the assist pass is taken into account, it becomes advantageous to help another player to score. If financial advisers are rewarded for bringing in new clients, they may be less interested in looking at the "leak" of nonloyal customers. If the reward system takes into account both new and loyal clients, financial advisers will behave accordingly.

To reinforce cooperation across departments in the case of airplane maintenance operations, two assessment criteria are simultaneously taken into consideration – measurement of quality at each operating step and total maintenance time – whatever incidents may arise during the check. When assessment systems give people knowledge of their interconnections, total maintenance time in this case, they perceive what must be changed and behave accordingly.

CONCLUSION

Translating a vision into action – changing the culture of an organization – does not just happen by decree. Change must be guided by a systematic process. What is important is a little inspiration – and a lot of perspiration and persistence.

CONCLUSION

Throughout the book I have tried to demonstrate how it is possible to look at any business with a simple pair of glasses, one lens focused on the product and operations in the back stage and the other on the market and the customer relationship in the front stage. When the two lenses are well focused, they give an integrated view, a relief map of the business, and the key issues appear more distinctly. Obviously, I have centered my attention on the front stage. But I think that in the future the back stage will become more open and visible. Where traditionally, manufacturing managers have sought to maximize efficiency and protect their operations from outside disturbances, the pressure from the market will make that stance less tenable. The back stage will be forced to become more open and more flexible, with more direct connections to marketing and strategic planning. As customers continue to become ever more present, their presence will influence the organization on deeper and deeper levels, penetrating the most remote areas and making the issue of back and front alignment even more crucial.

Although we may all be more or less in services now, we will be even more so in the future, as manufacturers will have to unleash the full service potential of their factories and capitalize on the complete range of services they can provide: the ability to construct prototypes quickly; the flexibility to adjust smoothly to more varied demands (mass customization); and the willingness to help customers with installation, maintenance and technical expertise. The future belongs to those who know how to create value that matters to the customer, and the back stage has a role to play.

On the other hand, the pressure of competition, the commoditization of products and services, the disaggregating of the value chain and the lowering of communication costs, render jobs and activities more standard and increase the strain on cost reduction. Outsourcing and offshoring have become part of everyday conversation and political debate. Many observers fear that any job that can be described and specified precisely will be either automated or dispatched abroad. Even "service" jobs that hitherto were not directly affected are now at risk.

According to a study conducted by the McKinsey Global Institute[1] "eleven percent of worldwide service employment could in theory be performed remotely." In this study, service employment refers to the service sector which is a confusing notion as explained in this book. The eleven percent applied to the whole sector does not have much meaning. The study reaches more interesting conclusions by breaking down the global economy into eight representative sectors and distinguishing at one end of the spectrum "packaged software and IT services" with an outsourcing potential of 49% and, at the other end, "healthcare" and "retail" with an outsourcing potential of 8% and 3% respectively.

This could be better explained with the front-stage definition of services. Nearly half of the employment in the "package software and IT services" could be resourced remotely because most activities are back stage, product centered. In contrast, "healthcare" and "retail" have more customer-facing service functions in the front stage. Some activities are done in the presence of the customer and it is hardly possible to export a surgical operation.

"You cannot export a haircut," explains Tom Friedman,[2] "but you could export the appointment part of it." Now, would you outsource it? Would you offshore your call center to India? This is a sensitive issue. It depends on the level of intimacy, quality of feedback, personalization or integration you want to keep with your customer. By now you should have useful ideas and concepts to help you answer this question.

The objective of this book was to find a valuable, simple and economic definition of services that could travel well across a number of businesses, combine nicely with different approaches and ideas already used to explore the field, and address the basic issues. This operational definition should help managers challenge their business and come rapidly to useful conclusions by using a number of related concepts and instruments.

I have unfolded the service definition on the service triangle to show the dual-partnership culture. I have analyzed the shift to commoditization and the need to position and reposition the service on the service-intensity matrix. I have shown the difficulty of designing and fitting the service mix to provide a good balance between value to customer, value to employee and value to firm. I have explored the three quality movements to show the specific aspects of service quality. I have tested the definition on two extreme examples, industrial services and professional services, to show the robustness of the concept.

I have tried to remain as sparing as possible with concepts, as I think there is an overdose of them in the literature, and that the most difficult part of the job is implementation. Concepts, maps and representations should help everyone challenge the status quo and start a dynamic of realignment within a proper change process. I have unfolded the service definition to explore the domain, and I hope you are convinced now that services should be considered as front-stage activities.

I follow the definition to the simple conclusion: we may all be in services now, more or less, but in the future, we shall be even more so.

NOTES

CHAPTER 1 – TOWARD A NEW DEFINITION OF SERVICES

1 Sources of data for pages on sector classification:
   - OECD Quarterly Labor Force Statistics
   - Mitchell, B.R. *International historical statistics: The Americas 1750–1993*. 4th edn. McMillan Reference, 1998. Table B1.
   - US Department of Labor. Bureau of Labor Statistics. *Employment, Hours, and Earnings* from the Current Employment Statistics survey (National).

2 Brown, Richard and Julius DeAnne. *Manufacturing in the New World Order: Shell International Petroleum Company*. Global Scenarios, 1993.

3 Theodore Levitt. "Production-line Approach to Service". *Harvard Business Review*, Sept/Oct 1972.

4 Galbraith, Jay. *Designing Organizations*. Jossey-Bass, 1995.

CHAPTER 2 – SERVICES: THE FRONT-STAGE EXPERIENCE

1 Normann, Richard. *Service Management: Strategy and Leadership in Service Business*. John Wiley & Sons, 3rd edn, 2000.

2 Baumol, William J. and Kenneth McLennan (eds). *Productivity Growth and United States Competitiveness*. Oxford University Press, 1985.

3 Carlzon, Jan. *Moments of Truth*. Ballinger Publishing Company, 1987.

4 Vandermerwe, Sandra. *From Tin Soldiers to Russian Dolls: Creating Added Value through Services*. Butterworth-Heinemann, 1993.

5 Welch, Jack. *Straight from the Gut*. Warren Books, 2001.

CHAPTER 3 – THE SERVICE TRIANGLE

1 Bandler, Richard and John Grinder. *Frogs into Princes: Neurolinguistic Programming*. Eden Grove Edns, 1990.

2   Heskett, James, Thomas Jones, Gary Loveman, Earl Sasser and Leonard Schlesinger. "Putting the Service–Profit Chain to Work". *Harvard Business Review*, March/April 1994.

CHAPTER 4 – THE SERVICE-INTENSITY MATRIX

1   McLuhan, Marshall. *Forward through the Rearview Mirror, Reflections on and by Marshall McLuhan*. The MIT Press, 1996.

2   Hayes, Robert and Steve Wheelwright. "Link Manufacturing Process and Product Life Cycles". *Harvard Business Review*, Jan/Feb 1979.

3   Maister, David. *Managing the Professional Service Firm*. The Free Press, 2003.

CHAPTER 5 – FINDING AND KEEPING THE FIT

1   Vandermerwe, Sandra. *From Tin Soldiers to Russian Dolls: Creating Added Value through Services*. Butterworth-Heinemann, 1993.

CHAPTER 7 – THE THREE MOVEMENTS OF QUALITY

1   Deming, Edward. *Out of the Crisis*. MIT Press, 1982.

2   Ishikawa, Kaoru. *What is Total Quality Control? The Japanese Way*. Prentice Hall, 1985.

3   Crosby, Philip. *Quality without Tears*. Plume Book, 1984.

4   Sewell, Carl. *Customers for Life*. Pocket Books, 1990.

5   Hammer, Michael and James Champy. *Re-engineering the Corporation*. Harper Business, 1994.

CHAPTER 8 – BALANCING SUPPLY AND DEMAND

1   Talluri, Kalyan and Garrett Van Ryzin. *Theory and Practice of Revenue Management*. Kluwer Academic Publishers, 2004.

2   Larson, Richard. "There's more to a line than its wait". *Technology Review*, July 1988.

CHAPTER 9 – FROM INDUSTRIAL TO PROFESSIONAL SERVICES

1   Vandermerwe, S. and M. Taishoff. *SKF Bearings: Market Orientation through Services*. IMD case study, 1991.

2   Kim, Chan and Renée Mauborgne. *Blue Ocean Strategy*. Harvard Business Press, 2005.

3   Welch, Jack. *Straight from the Gut*. Warner Books, 2001.

4   Scott, Mark C. *The Professional Service Firm*. John Wiley, 2001.

5   Maister, David. *True Professionalism*. The Free Press, 1997.

6 Oliva, Rogelio, Hallowell, Roger and Gabriel Bitran. *Merrill Lynch: Supernova*. Harvard Business Services case study 9-604-053, 2003.

CHAPTER 10 – MANAGING THE CHANGE PROCESS

1 Christensen, Clayton M. *The Innovator's Dilemma: When Technologies Cause Great Firms to Fail*. Harvard Business School Press, 1997.

CONCLUSION

1 McKinsey Global Institute. *The Emerging Global Labor Market*. 2005.

2 Friedman, Thomas. *The World is Flat*. Farrar, Strauss and Giroux, 2005.

BIBLIOGRAPHY ON SERVICES

Anderson, Kristin and Ron Zemke. *Knock your Socks Off: Delivering Service.* Amacom, 1991.

Bandler, Richard and John Grinder. *Frogs into Princes: Neurolinguistic Programming.* Eden Grove Edtns, 1990.

Bell, Chip R. and Ron Zemke. *Knock your Socks Off: Managing Service.* Amacom, 1992.

Berry, Leonard L., Parasuraman, A. and Valarie A. Zeithmal. "Servqual: A Multiple-Item Scale for Measuring Customer Perceptions of Service Quality". (Report No. 86-108), Marketing Science Institute, 1986.

Berry, Leonard L. *On Great Service: A Framework for Action.* The Free Press, 1995.

Berry, Leonard L. *Discovering the Soul of Service: The Nine Drivers of Sustainable Business Success.* Free Press, 1999.

Brown, Richard and Julius DeAnne. *Manufacturing in the New World Order: Shell International Petroleum Company.* Global Scenarios, 1993.

Carlzon, Jan. *Moments of Truth.* Ballinger Publishing Company, 1987.

Christensen, Clayton M. *The Innovator's Dilemma: When Technologies Cause Great Firms to Fail.* Harvard Business School Press, 1997.

Collier, David A. *Service Management: The Automation of Services.* Prentice-Hall, 1985.

Collier, David A. *Service Management: Operating Decisions.* Prentice-Hall, 1987.

Crosby, Philip B. *Quality without Tears: The Art of Hassle-Free Management.* Plume Book, 1984.

Deming, Edward. *Out of the Crisis.* MIT Press, 1982.

Edvardsson, Bo, Thomasson, Bertil and John Øvretveit. *Quality of Service: Making It Really Work.* McGraw-Hill, 1994.

Fitzsimmons, James A. and Mona J. Fitzsimmons. *Service Management: Operations, Strategy, and Information Technology.* 4th edn, McGraw-Hill Irwin, 2004.

Freemantle, David. *Incredible Customer Service:The Final Test.* McGraw-Hill, 1993.

Friedman, Thomas. *The World is Flat.* Farrar, Straus & Giroux, New York, 2005.

Galbraith, Jay R. *Designing Organizations: An Executive Briefing on Strategy, Structure and Process.* Jossey-Bass, 1995.

Gee, Francesca and James Teboul. *Benihana U.K. (Ltd.).* INSEAD case study, 1997.

Gladwell, Malcolm. *The Tipping Point.* Blackday Books, 2000.

Grönroos, Christian. *Service Management and Marketing: Managing the Moments of Truth in Service Competition.* Lexington Books, 1990.

Grönroos, Christian. *Service Management and Marketing: a Customer Relationship Management Approach.* 2nd edn, Wiley, 2000.

Hammer, Michael and James Champy. *Re-engineering the Corporation.* Harper Business, 1994.

Hart, Christopher W.L. "The Power of Unconditional Service Guarantees". *Harvard Business Review,* July/August 1988.

Hart, Christopher W.L., Heskett, James L. and W. Earl Sasser, Jr. "The Profitable Art of Service Recovery". *Harvard Business Review,* July/August 1990, pp. 148–56.

Hayes, Robert H. and Steven C. Wheelwright. "Link Manufacturing Process and Product Life Cycles". *Harvard Business Review,* Jan/Feb 1979.

Heskett, James L. *Shouldice Hospital Limited.* Harvard Business Services case study, 1989.

Heskett, James L., Jones, Thomas O., Loveman, Gary W., Sasser, Jr., Earl W. and Leonard A. Schlesinger. "Putting the Service–Profit Chain to Work". *Harvard Business Review,* March/April 1994, pp. 164–74.

Heskett, James L., Sasser, Jr., Earl W. and Christopher W.L. Hart. *Service Breakthroughs: Changing the Rules of the Game.* The Free Press, 1990.

Heskett, James L., Sasser, Jr., Earl W. and Leonard A. Schlesinger. *The Service–Profit Chain: How Leading Companies Link Profit and Growth to Loyalty, Satisfaction, and Value.* The Free Press, 1997.

Imai, Massaki. *Gemba Kaizen: A Commonsense, Low-Cost Approach to Management.* McGraw-Hill, 1997.

Ishikawa, Kaoru. *What is Total Quality Control? The Japanese Way.* Prentice-Hall, 1985.

Kim, Chan and Renée Mauborgne. *Blue Ocean Strategy: How to Create Uncontested Market Space and Make Competition Irrelevant.* Harvard Business Press, 2005.

Kotter, John P. *Leading Change.* Harvard Business School Press, 1996.

Larson, Richard. "There's More to a Line Than its Wait". *Technology Review,* July 1988.

Levitt, Theodore. "The Industrialization of Service". *Harvard Business Review,* Sept/Oct 1976, pp. 63–74.

Levitt, Theodore. "Production-line Approach to Service". *Harvard Business Review,* Sept/Oct 1972, pp. 41–52.

Lovelock, Christopher H. *Product Plus: How Product + Service = Competitive Advantage.* McGraw-Hill, 1993.

Lovelock, Christopher H. and Jochen Wirtz. *Services Marketing: People, Technology, Strategy.* Prentice Hall, 2003.

Maister, David H. *True Professionalism: The Courage to Care About Your People, Your Clients, and Your Career.* The Free Press, 1997.

Maister, David H. *Managing the Professional Service Firm.* The Free Press, 2003.

McLuhan, Marshall. *Forward through the Rearview Mirror, Reflections on and by Marshall McLuhan.* The MIT Press, 1996.

Normann, Richard. *Service Management: Strategy and Leadership in Service Business.* 3rd edn, John Wiley & Sons, 2000.

Oliva, Rogelio, Hallowell, Roger and Gabriel Bitran. *Merrill Lynch: Supernova.* Harvard Business Services case study 9-604-053, 2003.

Pasuraman, A. and Leonard L. Berry. *Marketing Services: Competing Through Quality.* Free Press, 2004.

Payne, Adrian. *The Essence of Services Marketing.* Prentice Hall, 1993.

Pine II, B. Joseph and James H. Gilmore. *The Experience Economy: Work is Theater & Every Business a Stage.* Harvard Business School Press, 1999.

Quinn, James Brian. *Intelligent Enterprise.* The Free Press, 1992.

Quinn, James Brian and Christopher E. Gagnon. "Will Services Follow Manufacturing into Decline?" *Harvard Business Review,* November/December 1986, pp. 95–103.

Reichheld, Frederick F. and W. Earl Sasser, Jr. ; "Zero Defections: Quality Comes to Services". *Harvard Business Review,* September/October 1990, pp. 105–11.

Rust, Roland T. and Richard L. Oliver (eds). *Service Quality: New Directions in Theory and Practice.* SAGE Publications, 1994.

Schlesinger, Leonard A. and James L. Heskett. "The Service-Driven Service Company". *Harvard Business Review,* September/October 1991, pp. 71–81.

Schmidt, Waldemar, Adler, Gordon and Els van Weering. *Winning at Service: Lessons from Service Leaders.* Wiley, 2003.

Schneider, Benjamin and David E. Bowen. *Winning the Service Game.* Harvard Business School Press, 1995.

Scott, Marc. *The Professional Service Firm.* Wiley, 2001.

Sewell, Carl. *Customers for Life.* Pocket Books, 1990.

Shostack, G. Lynn. "Breaking Free from Product Marketing". *Journal of Marketing,* April 1977, pp. 73–80.

Shostack, G. Lynn. "Designing Services That Deliver". *Harvard Business Review,* January/February 1984, pp. 133–9.

Talluri, Kalyan and Garrett J. Van Ryzin. *The Theory and Practice of Revenue Management.* Kluwer Academic Publishers, 2004.

Teboul, James. *Managing Quality Dynamics*. Prentice Hall, 1991.

Vandermerwe, Sandra. *From Tin Soldiers to Russian Dolls: Creating Added Value through Services*. Butterworth-Heinemann, 1993.

Vandermerwe, Sandra. *The Eleventh Commandment: Transforming to "Own" Customers*. John Wiley & Sons, 1996.

Vandermerwe, S. and M. Taishoff. *SKF Bearings: Market Orientation through Services*. IMD case study, 1991.

Van Looy, Bart, Roland Van Dierdonck and Paul Gemmel (eds). *Service Management: an Integrated Approach*. Financial Times Publishing, 1998.

Watkins, Michael. *The First 90 Days: Critical Success Strategies for New Leaders at All Levels*. Harvard Business School Press, 2003.

Welch, Jack. *Straight from the Gut*. Warner Books, 2001.

Wright, Lauren and Christopher H. Lovelock. *Principles of Service Marketing and Management*. Prentice Hall, 2004.

Wyckoff, Daryl. "New Tools for Achieving Service Quality". *The Cornell HRA Quarterly*, November 1984.

Zeithaml, Valarie, Parasuraman, A. and Leonard L. Berry. *Delivering Quality Service: Balancing Customer Perceptions and Expectations*. The Free Press, 1990.

Zeithaml, Valarie and Mary Bitner. *Services Marketing*. McGraw, 2002.

INDEX

A

Accenture, 120–2
Accor
   see hotel(s)
account manager, 22, 34
accounting
   big four accounting firms,
      120, 121
activity, activities
   customer activity cycle, 64
   insourcing activities, 118,
      119
adopters
   early adopters, 133–5
Air Liquide, 2, 21, 116, 117
Air Products, 20
airline companies
   British Airways, 90
   Scandinavian Airlines, 26
   SouthWest Airlines, 91
   Virgin Atlantic Airlines, 68
alignment
   alignment stage, 138
   process alignment, 19, 93
Aoki, Rocky, 49, 59, 62
appraisal costs, 81
approach
   black-box approach, 12
   cheese slicer approach, 81
   relational approach, 27
   silo approach, 92
   transactional approach, 31,
      32
ATM, 51

B

batch
   see production
Baumol, William, 23
Bearing Services Division, 114,
   131
benchmark, benchmarking, 97,
   130
benefits
   perceived benefits, 58, 72
Benihana, Benihana of Tokyo
   see restaurants
bias
   confirmation bias, 73
big bang, 95, 96
billable hours, time, 122, 123
black-box
   see approach
boilermaker, 34, 35
Boston Consulting Group, 120
Boston's Beth Israel Hospital
   see hospitals
bottleneck(s), 46, 103, 109
bow-tie
   see relationship(s)
brain
   see project
Branson, Richard, 68
breakthrough
   see service
British Airways
   see airline companies
broker, brokerage
   brokerage business, 124
   discount broker, 53, 123–5

full-service brokerage, 123,
    124
internet brokerage, 52
online broker, 123, 124, 130
retail brokerage, 123
Brown, Richard, 5
Browning-Singlemann
    see classification
BPR
    see Business Process
        Reengineering
business
    business integration, 55, 121
    business process(es), 77, 92,
        93, 121, 128
    business traveler(s), 101, 106
Business Process Reengineering,
    BPR, 128
business-to-business
    see service

C

Caesar, Julius, 130
call center, 23, 26, 53, 66, 84,
    85, 102, 125
Cap Gemini, 121
capacity
    capacity flexibility, 104, 105
    capacity utilization, 46, 58,
        59, 61–3, 95, 99, 102
    flexible capacity, 104, 105
    idle capacity, 99, 100, 109
    overcapacity, 103, 127
    sharing capacity, 105
    undercapacity, 103
car distribution, 21
Carlzon, Jan, 26
categories
    see service
categorization, 73
chain
    see service
    see value
Champy, James, 96
change acceleration process,
    77, 128

chart
    see flow
cheese slicer
    see approach
Christensen, Clayton, 132
claim
    see insurance
classification
    Browning-Singlemann
        classification, 7
    three-sector classification, 1,
        4, 9
clicks
    clicks and mortar, 53, 54
coach, coaches, coaching, 37,
    38, 122, 123
coalition
    guiding coalition, 131
comfort zone, 129–31
committee
    steering committee, 131,
        135–7
commodity, commodities,
    commoditization, 7, 20, 41,
    42, 45, 47, 63, 64, 113, 115,
    121, 123–5, 127, 130, 140,
    141
complaint(s)
    see customer
conformity
    see product
consolidation
    see stage
consultancies, 120, 122
consulting
    consulting business(es), 54,
        55
    consulting firm, 120
consumer durables, 20, 21
contact
    face-to-face contact, 22, 43,
        50, 51, 125
    online contact, 22, 52, 53,
        99, 124, 125
continuous
    see flow
control
    see process

co-produce, co-producers, co-
   production, 25, 29, 36, 37,
   42, 43, 51, 53, 56, 65, 104
cost(s)
   appraisal costs, 81
   cost of non-conformance, 82
   cost of overcapacity, 103,
      127
   cost of quality, 81, 82
   cost of undercapacity, 103
   cost-per-mile solution, 98
   external failure costs, 82
   failure costs, 81, 82
   internal failure costs, 81, 82
   prevention costs, 81
cross-selling, 29, 39, 90, 126
cross-trained, 105
cultural mindset, 112
customer(s)
   customer account teams, 98
   customer activity cycle, 64
   customer-centered
      measures, 98
   customer complaint, 88, 89
   customer loyalty, 38
   customer segmentation, 56
   customer–supplier interface,
      92
   customer–supplier
      relationships, 93
   internal customers, 29, 92,
      93
   leisure customers, 106
   local customer support, 117,
      118
   loyal customers, 37, 89, 90,
      101, 139
   value of customer, 89
   voice of the customer, 77,
      91, 92
customization
   mass customization, 47, 140
cycle
   customer activity cycle, 64
   cycle time, 43, 62, 96, 137
   value creation cycle, 21, 64,
      65, 67, 69, 113–17, 127
   value cycle, 67, 68

D

Dalkey, Norman, 100
dealership
   truck dealership, 98
DeAnne, Julius, 5
decision(s)
   operating decisions, 58, 61
defect(s)
   see zero
defection(s)
   see zero
delivery
   delivery gap, 71, 72, 74, 75
   service delivery, 12, 14, 28,
      38, 63, 74
Delphi
   see method(s)
demand
   centralized demand, 102
   complementary demand,
      102
   scheduling demand, 101
   seasonal demand, 100
   shifting demand, 101, 102
   smoothing demand, 102,
      103, 105
   storing demand, 102
Deming, Edward, 79
deployment
   see stage
design, redesign
   design gap, 70–2, 74–6
   modular design, 30, 47
   product design, 67
   redesign, 42, 64, 95, 97
deviation
   standard deviation, 24, 78,
      79
diagram
   cause-and-effect diagram, 80
   fishbone diagram, 80, 83, 84
diamond
   see relationship
differentiation
   postponed differentiation, 47
diffusion
   see model

dimension
    people dimension, 43, 50,
      51, 56
    process dimension, 43, 50,
      51, 56
    product dimension, 41, 42,
      56
discount
    see broker
discount seat allocation, 106
distribution
    distribution networks, 26, 29
dual
    dual partnership culture, 2,
      35, 39, 40, 141

E

eBay, 37
e-business, 50, 52, 53, 123
e-service(s), 51
eater-tainement, 62, 64
Economist, The, 4
economy, economies
    economy(ies) of relationship,
      29, 90
    economy(ies) of scale, 4, 15,
      16, 18, 20, 23, 60, 46, 47,
      50, 68
    economy(ies) of scope, 29,
      90
EDS, 121
end
    back end, 17, 18
    front end, 16, 17, 18
    front-end function, 21
    front-end structure, 16
error
    see trial
excellence
    see product
expectations, 26, 66, 74, 75,
    77, 84–8, 111
    after-sale experience, 22, 33
    experience, 9, 12, 13
    memorable experience,
      58–60

    pre-sale experience, 33
    sales experience, 22
    seamless experience, 29, 92,
      97, 98
    service experience, 13, 15,
      57, 87
expert
    see system(s)

F

face-to-face
    see contact
factor
    seasonality factor, 100
    utilization factor, 109, 110
factory
    factory-style, 19
failure
    external failure costs, 82
    failure costs, 80–2
    internal failure costs, 81
Financial Advisory Center, 125
fish farmer, 21
fishbone
    see diagram
flexibility, flexible
    capacity flexibility, 104
    flexibility, 95
    flexible capacity, 105
    flexible production lines, 30
    flexible workshop, 30
flow
    continuous flow, 45–7
    flow chart, 94, 96, 103
focus
    focus operations, 95
followers, 133, 134, 136, 138
Formule 1
    see hotel(s)
frame
    frame of reference, 72, 74,
      87
full service
    see service

G

gap
  delivery gap, 71, 72, 74, 75
  perception gap, 71, 72
  quality gap, 2, 70, 127
  value gap, 75–7, 86
gatekeepers, 33, 34, 133, 136
General Electric, 114, 118
General Motors, 11
gray hair
  see project

H

hairdresser, 7, 43
hamburger-flippers, 7
Hammer, Michael, 96
Hayes, Bob, 45
Helmer, Olaf, 100
Heskett, James, 38
hospitals
  Boston's Beth Israel Hospital,
    97
  Shouldice Hospital, 57, 103,
    108
hotels
  Accor Group, hotels, 44
  Formule 1, 44, 67
  full-service hotel, 65, 66
  Marriott hotels, 44
  Ritz-Carlton, 35, 44, 85, 89

I

IBM Credit Corporation, 96
idle
  see capacity
improvement
  see process
incident report form, 89
index
  service quality index, 88
  industrialization,
    industrialize,

industrializing, 12, 15, 20,
    23
inguinal hernia, 57, 58
innovators, 133–5
insourcing
  see activities
insurance
  insurance claim, 94
  Progressive Insurance, 88
intangible, 13, 24, 27, 29, 87,
    114
integration
  business integration, 17, 55,
    121
  integration, 25, 29, 55, 141
  integration mechanisms, 30
  systems integration, 55,
    121
integrator(s), 121
intensity
  intensity of interaction, 34,
    41–3
  service-intensity matrix, 2,
    41, 123, 127, 141
intensive
  information-intensive
    services, 113
  intensive, 20, 22
  service-intensive goods, 20
interaction, interactive
  face-to-face interaction, 52
  intensity of interaction, 34
  interaction, 13, 16, 19, 22–4,
    26–8, 31, 33, 37
  interactive relationships, 27
  seamless interaction, 25, 53
internal
  internal customers, 29, 92,
    93
  internal marketing, 29, 32,
    36

J

Jobs, Steve, 41

K

Kaizen, 77, 128
knowledge
  see management

L

labor
  division of labor, 24, 25, 29,
    94, 111
laggards, 133
law
  law firm, 23, 42, 122
  law of authority, 93
  law of the situation, 93
leader(s)
  opinion leader(s), 133–5
leverage
  expertise leverage, 43
  leverage of professional time,
    122
  leverage ratio, 122
Levitt, Theodore, 14, 15
lifetime
  see value
line(s)
  flexible production lines, 30
  line production, 45, 47
  product line, 131
  production line(s), 15, 30,
    45–8
  waiting lines, 15, 102,
    108–12
loyal, loyalty
  customer loyalty, 38
  loyal customer, 37, 89, 90,
    101

M

Maister, David, 54, 123
management
  knowledge management,
    55, 123, 139
  revenue management, 106,
    108
  Time-Based Management,
    128
  yield management, 106,
    108
market, marketer(s), marketing
  aftermarket, 115–17, 131
  before market, 115
  internal marketing, 29, 32,
    36
  market space, 62, 64
  marketing mix, 26, 27, 29,
    31, 34, 40, 102
  part-time marketer(s), 28
  product marketing, 32
  service marketing, 32
  transactional marketing, 27,
    29
Marriott hotels
  see hotels
Marx, Karl, 7
mass
  mass customization, 47, 140
  mass production, 20, 23, 24,
    115
matrix
  process matrix, 45, 48, 49
  product matrix, 45, 48, 49
  service-intensity matrix, 41,
    43, 45, 48–50, 52–7, 120,
    123, 127, 141
McDonald's
  see restaurants
McKinsey Global Institute, 120,
  121, 141
McLuhan, Marshall, 45
medical oxygen, 114
medium
  the medium is the message,
    45
Merrill Lynch, 52, 53, 124, 125,
  130
method(s)
  analogy method, 100
  Delphi method, 100
  explanatory method(s), 100

mix
  marketing mix, 26, 27, 29,
    31, 34, 40, 102
  service mix, 2, 27–9, 34, 40,
    41, 45, 57–9, 68–70, 112,
    122, 141
mode
  pull mode, 138
  push mode, 138
model
  diffusion model, 133
  three-sector model, 1, 4, 9
modular
  modular design, 30, 47
mortar
  see clicks
moving
  moving average, 100
multiskilled, 60–2, 95, 97, 105,
  111

N

network, networks
  distribution network(s), 26,
    29
no show(s), 102
no win, no fee, 35
nominal
  nominal value, 78–80
nonbillable hours, time, 123

O

offshore(d), offshoring, 48, 141
online
  online business(es), 23
  online communications, 26
onshore(d), onshoring , 48, 141
operations
  focus operations, 95
opinion
  opinion leader(s), 133–5
organization
  functional organization, 45,
    46, 49

outsource(d), outsourcing, 8, 9,
  18, 30
  outsourcing activities, 48,
    104, 140, 141
overbooking, 102, 103, 106–8
overcapacity, 103, 127
  see also cost
overgeneralization, 73, 74
owner
  see process

P

the four P's, 26, 27
the six P's, 27, 57
partnership
  dual partnership culture, 2,
    35, 39, 40, 141
part-time
  see marketers
patient
  value to patients, 58
peer
  see pressure
perceived
  see benefits, sacrifices
perception
  see gap
performance, 13, 22, 25, 27,
  29, 38, 113, 114, 118, 128,
  131, 134, 137–9
pressure
  peer pressure, 138
prevention
  see cost
primary nurse, 98
process(es)
  business process(es), 77, 92,
    93, 121
  Business Process
    Reengineering, 77, 128
  change acceleration process,
    77, 128
  process alignment, 91, 93
  process control, 79, 80, 83,
    85
  process dimension, 43

process improvement, 93,
    94, 131
process owner, 93, 95, 97
process redesign, 95, 97
process reengineering, 98
production process(es), 19,
    28, 45, 78
processing of information, 15,
    24, 48
producer
    see services
product
    product conformity, 29, 76,
        98
    product dimension, 41, 42,
        78
    product excellence, 16, 20,
        23, 29, 31
    product line, 131
    product marketing, 32
    product plus, 113, 115, 118
    product segmentation, 57
    pure product, 12, 13, 29
    quality of product, 2, 70, 76
    tangible product, 27, 77
production
    batch production, 45, 47
    line production, 45, 47
    mass production, 20, 23, 24,
        115
    production line, 15, 30, 45–8
    production process(es), 19,
        28, 45, 78
productivity, 22, 23, 31, 38, 39,
    43, 45, 61, 62, 88, 90, 126
profit
    see service
Progressive
    see insurance
project
    brain project, 54, 55, 121
    gray hair project, 54, 55, 121
    procedure project, 55, 121
    proof of the pudding, 85,
        86
proposition
    see service

pure
    pure goods, 20
    pure product, 12, 13, 29
    pure service, 12, 13, 20, 22,
        23, 27, 29, 119
pyramid
    turning the pyramid, 37

Q

quality, qualitative
    cost of quality, 81, 82
    qualitative techniques, 100
    quality gap, 2, 70, 127
    quality of product, 2, 70, 76
    quality of service, 2, 70, 76,
        99, 112
    service quality index, 88
    Total Quality Control, TQC,
        128
    Total Quality Management,
        TQM, 77, 128
queue(s), 25, 29, 99, 105,
    108–12
    see also waiting line(s)

R

rainmakers, 122
rate(s)
    arrival rate(s), 109
    service rate(s), 109
realignment, 95, 103, 127, 142
recover(ed), recovery, 22, 26,
    29, 37, 58, 72, 80, 88, 89,
    91, 116
reengineering, 93, 95, 98
reference
    see frame
referral(s), 39, 126
relational
    see approach
relationship(s)
    bow tie relationship, 33
    customer relationship(s), 17,
        27, 140

diamond relationship, 33
interactive relationships, 27
satisfactory relationship, 28
reservation
see systems
resister(s), resistor(s), 82, 133,
138
restaurant(s)
Benihana, 59, 60–4
fast-food restaurant, 11, 42,
46, 48–50, 104, 105
gourmet restaurant, 13, 15,
48–50
McDonald's, 12, 15, 84
restaurant business, 48–50,
64
retail
see broker, brokerage
retail bank(s), 42, 47
revenue
see management
right
right thing, 77, 85–7, 91, 98
thing right, 77–9, 82, 91, 98
Ritz-Carlton hotel
see hotels
Rolls-Royce, 117
Rubicon River, 130

S

sacrifices
perceived sacrifices, 58, 72
sale
after-sale(s) experience, 22,
33, 34
pre-sale(s) experience, 33,
34
scale
see economy
Scandinavian Airlines
see airline companies
scheduling, 46, 101, 105
Schwab, Charles, 53, 123, 124
scope
see economy
Scott, Mark, 119

seamless
see experience
see interaction
seasonal, seasonality
seasonal demand, 95, 99,
100
seasonal variation,100
seasonality factor, 100
sector(s)
activity sector(s), 20
economic sector, 7, 20
industrial sector, 4, 5, 11, 16,
22, 23, 115
manufacturing sector, 5
primary sector, 4
secondary sector, 4
service sector, 1, 4–7, 11, 14,
22, 23, 141
tertiary sector, 4, 10
three-sector model, 4, 9, 12,
19
segmentation
customer segmentation, 56
product segmentation, 57
Service Master, 118
service(s)
breakthrough service(s), 2,
59, 62
business-to-business
service(s), 8, 9, 33, 39,
115
consumer service(s), 9
distributive service(s), 8, 10
e-service(s), 51
financial service(s), 41, 52,
53, 123, 124
full service, 52, 57, 65, 66,
116–18, 123–5, 140
industrial service(s), 2, 113,
142
information-intensive
service(s), 20, 22
nonmarketed service(s),
8–11
personal service(s), 8, 10, 11,
23
producer service(s), 8–11

professional service(s), 2, 112, 113, 119, 120, 142
progressive service(s), 23
pure service(s), 12, 13, 20, 22, 23, 27, 29, 119
quality of service, 2, 70, 76, 99, 112
self-service(s), 8, 9, 15, 43, 50, 67
service categories, 23
service delivery, 12, 14, 28, 38, 63, 74
service-intensity matrix, 41, 43, 45, 48–50, 52–7
service-intensive good(s), 20
service marketing, 32
service mix, 2, 27–9, 34, 40, 41, 45, 57–9, 68–70, 112, 122, 141
service–profit chain, 38
service proposition, 2, 55–7, 59–66, 114, 116, 117, 127, 130
service quality index, 88
service sector, 1, 4–7, 11, 14, 22, 23, 141
service triangle, 2, 28, 31, 32, 38–40, 56, 58, 63, 70, 76, 119, 141
service utilization, 101
stagnant service(s), 23
unbundled service(s), 116
value-added service(s), 52, 124
servitude, 6
Sewell, Carl, 80
Shouldice Hospital
    see hospitals
Six Sigma, 128
silo
    see approach
SKF, 115–17, 131, 132, 136
Smith, Adam, 7
solution
    cost-per-mile solution, 98
SouthWest Airlines
    see airline companies

specialization, 9, 23–5, 29, 94, 96
stage
    alignment stage, 138
    consolidation stage, 134, 138, 139
    deployment stage, 134, 136
    initiation stage, 134
    standardization, 23, 24, 29, 43, 48, 58, 84
statement
    mission statement, 132
Statistical Process Control, SPC, 79, 81
steering committee, 131, 135–7
superstore(s), 53, 54
Sushi Doraku, 64
symmetry
    symmetry of roles, 36
systems
    expert system(s), 51, 55
    reservation system(s), 99, 102, 106, 110
    systems integration, 121

T

tangible
    see product
techniques
    qualitative techniques, 100
time
    billable time, 122, 123
    cycle time, 43, 62, 96, 137
    leverage of professional time, 122
    Time-Based Management, 128
tolerance(s)
    tolerance limits, 78
    Total Quality Control (TQC)
        see quality
Total Quality Management (TQM)
    see quality

Toyota, 22
transactional
   see also approach, marketing
transformation, 12, 14, 19, 21,
   24, 25, 35, 121, 122
trend
   basic trend, 100
   trend extension, 100
trial
   trial and error, 81
triangle
   see service
truck dealership, 98
truth
   moment(s) of truth, 19, 26,
      29, 64, 66, 83, 88
turnaround, 127

U

undercapacity, 103
   see also cost
underutilization, 99, 100
urgency
   sense of urgency, 129, 130,
      132, 133
utilization
   capacity utilization, 46, 58,
      59, 61–3, 95, 99, 102
   service utilization, 101
   utilization factor, 109, 110

V

value
   lifetime value, 90
   nominal value, 78–80
   value analysis, 67, 94
   value chain, 55, 121, 140
   value creation cycle, 21, 64,
      65, 67, 69, 113–17, 127
   value cycle, 67, 68
   value gap, 75–7, 86
   value to business, 61–3, 66
   value to customer(s), 58, 59,
      60, 63, 66, 69, 142

value to employee(s), 61, 63,
   66, 69, 142
value to patient(s), 58
value to the hospital, 58
value to the staff, 58
Vandemerwe, Sandra, 27, 64
vanilla
   vanilla commodity
      businesses, 42
variable(s)
   dependent variable, 100
   independent variable, 100
variation
   seasonal variation, 100
   variation limits, 79, 80
vertical
   vertical efficiency, 92
Virgin Atlantic Airlines
   see airline companies
voice
   see customer

W

waiting line(s), queue(s)
   average length of the queue,
      109, 110
   multiple queues, 111
   queue(s), 25, 29, 99,
      108–10, 112
   single queue, 110, 111
   take a number queue, 111
   waiting line(s), 15, 102,
      108–12
waste, 55, 62, 92–5, 127, 130
water distribution company,
   113, 114
Wealth of Nations, The, 7
Welch, Jack, 30, 118
Wheelwright, Steve, 45
willingness to pay, 58–60, 75,
   137
win(s)
   first wins, 129, 134
   no win, no fee, 35
wing-to-wing engine
   maintenance, 98

word of mouth, 27, 28, 36, 39,
40, 74, 75, 90, 126, 136
workshop, 30, 45, 48

Y

yield
see management

Z

zero
zero defections, 26, 29
zero defects, 24, 26, 77–9,
98
zone
comfort zone, 129–31